ANCHOR BOOKS

FLIGHTS OF FANCY

Edited by

Rachael Radford

First published in Great Britain in 2003 by
ANCHOR BOOKS
Remus House,
Coltsfoot Drive,
Peterborough, PE2 9JX
Telephone (01733) 898102

All Rights Reserved

Copyright Contributors 2002

HB ISBN 1 84418 084 0
SB ISBN 1 84418 085 9

FOREWORD

Anchor Books is a small press, established in 1992, with the aim of promoting readable poetry to as wide an audience as possible.

We hope to establish an outlet for writers of poetry who may have struggled to see their work in print.

The poems presented here have been selected from many entries, and as always editing proved to be a difficult task.

I trust this selection will delight and please the authors and all those who enjoy reading poetry.

Rachael Radford
Editor

CONTENTS

20 20 20 Something Vision	R Gibson	1
The Song	Miriam Mason	2
A Lifetime's Hobby	E D Bowen	4
My Daughter At Lamorna	Isabel (Liz) Samwells	5
Poltesco Vale	Nicolette A Bodilly	6
Guilt	Claire Willis	8
Is There Hope?	Kevin Dixon	9
Scarborough	Hannah E Finnegan	10
Steel Giants	Maureen Gilbert	11
My Thoughts	M G Clements	12
Is It Time?	David Sim	13
Copped	Jean Naseby	14
Bullies	Ruth Sayada	15
A Childhood Dream	L Cliffe	16
The Trout Fishing Challenge	K E Evans	17
A Sudden Storm	Eddie Main	18
SAD	Steve Urwin	19
The River Wye	Mary Hughes	20
Life's Pattern	May Morrott	21
Lilith Fay, Daughter Of The Moon	Jonathan Pegg	22
Marina	Peter James O'Rourke	23
On Stage	Lydia Barnett	24
Life	Douglas Bryan Kennett	25
The Market Square Dance	Stan Coombs	26
An Ill Wind	Christine Campbell	28
The Bargain Hunter	Tracey Ibbotson	29
Agricultural Heritage	Cherry Thacker	30
They	Christine DuPlessis	31
New Forest Hush	R Ansell	32
Famine	Michelle Rae	33
Grave Experience At St Edburg's	Kenneth John Webb	34
The Alternative	Gertrude Black	35
A New Day - A New Life	Ruth Newlands	36
Here I Am . . .	Marion McGarrigle	37
Tongue-In-Cheek	Eveline Weighell	38

Title	Author	Page
A Big Fat Ugly Day	Peggy Kelso	39
The Penalty King	Haley Frisby	40
We Don't Need People	Julie Currell	41
The Love Goddess	John Franks	42
My City	Maureen Kimpriktzis	43
The Garden Of Millennia	Sarah Johns	44
The Angler	Neilea Hames	45
Careless	Leita Donn	46
End Of The Line	Judith Hill	48
Sunshine Sue	Anne Haggarty (Angelena)	50
Ageing Pebbles	Robin E Edwards	51
Strangers In Town	Sue Cooper	52
Old Man	Clive White	53
The Most Important Things	Morag Kilpatrick	54
A Poem Dedicated To The Wright Stuff	Suzanne Reeves	55
My Norfolk	E Barker	56
Restlessness	J M Jones	57
My Old Garden Shed	Derek Harvey	58
Who Cares?	Keith Vaughan	60
Watchful Eye	Leona McNicholl	61
Harriet's New Home	Frances Roberts	62
Sunset	Elizabeth Maria Rait	64
To A Woman Growing Older	Margaret Munro Gibson	65
Expiry Date	Joyce Evans	66
Palms And Burnt Ashes	Russell Phillips	67
Friends	Sandra Hughes	68
An Unseen Friend	Victoria Louise Man	69
Surprise View	Dorothy Brown	70
The Star	Dareni	71
Doon At Rossay Fair	Jenny Brown	72
The Simple Man	Allan McFadyean	74
A Seventeenth Wedding Anniversary	Andrew A Duncan	75
Newspaper Shut-Down	Andrew Sanders	76
A Visit To The Bank	Paul Kelly	77
A Book Of Poems	Edna D'Lima	78
Boy Racer - An Essex Tale	Jon Oyster	79

Title	Author	Page
Old Vienna	H Willmott	80
Student Daughter	Trish Duxbury	81
Untitled	Bonnie Middleton	82
A Child's Country Dream	Carol Boneham	83
What Did I Do?	Laura Perkins	84
Ain't Life A Bitch!	Pam Tucker	85
Find Time	James W Bull	86
A Visit To Howarth	Molly A Kean	87
Ideal Weight	Rebecca H Weir	88
Thank You Tony Blair	Rachel Hobson	89
Journeying Forward, Looking Back	Susan Gale	90
Tea Break	Mike Jackson	91
The Driving Test	Marion Scarlett	92
Imagine	Alan Green	94
A Day's Journey	Daphne Clarke	95
Working In The Coal Mine	Audrey Machon Grayson	96
Landscape	Muriel Hughes	97
Goodbye	Steffen AP Lloyd	98
Time	Daniel P Taggart	99
Happy To Be	Sharon Brown	100
Terry Casement	Leigh-Ann Sloan	101
A Lady	R Tate	102
Untitled	M Simpson	103
The Neighbour	N V Wright	104
The Day You Were Born	A Hunter	105
Without Him	E J Prout	106
Foot And Mouth Disease	Robert Allen	108
Pain	Andrew Crump	109
Firelight Pictures	J Packwood	110
Norman's Lament	Ben Wolfe	112
Conscience	Tim Coburn	114
In The Name Of Religion	Margaret P Thomas	115
Life Within Light	Elaine Nicholas-Chan	116
12:24 To Deansgate	Heather Olly	118
The Gift	Doreen Wilkinson	119
Hooray	Anita Layland	120
Warbird	Raymond Hill	121

I Love The Night	C A Keohane-Johnson	122
The Family's Lament	Marjorie Seaman	123
A True 'Storey'	Sarah Smeaton	124
The Lady Of The Jaguar	E Davies	125
Time - Life's Predator	Sheila Storr	126
The Injection	Sue Starling	127
The End Of Freedom	Ann Nunan	128
You Are Not Alone!	H Doidge	129
Dire Warning - Never Jump To Conclusions	Reg Windett	130
The Trials And Tribulations Of A Diabetic Cat	Sue MacKenzie	132
The Meal	Mick Vukasinovic	133
Two Thousand	Vera May Waterworth	134
My Dog	Margaret R Bromham	135
Misti!	Linda Gregory	136
The Musical Box	Janet (Tuthill) Carter	137
Famous Bits	Val Hoare	138
Loving Kiss	Joanne Mills	140
Follow Your Dream	Cathy Mearman	141
Feet	Janet Degnan	142
Life As A Carer	B M Attwood	143
Council Conundrum	P A Greenwood	144
British Isles	Clarence Gascoigne	145
The Pain Game	Lynda Jobling	146
A Kentish Lad	Graham Bloss	147
Fishing Beach Hythe	Jax Burgess	148
All Sunday's Children	Glynis Flewin Cooke	149
Infinity	Margery Crabtree	150
A Summer Morn	I T Hoggan	152
Thank You!	Andrea Darling	153
Living With Angels	Vicky Stevens	154
The Dance Of Spring	Ronald D Lush	155
Treasure Trove	Paff	156
Ducklings	Win Price	157
Mother	Thelma (Slee) Thomas	158
Adam And Eve	Daisy Cooper	159
Teenage Kicks	Joanne Cross	160

Title	Author	Page
Bonnie, Clyde And Accomplices	Annette Murphy	161
Matt Cain	Coleen Bradshaw	162
The Furry Hat	Eveline Tucker	163
The Tiny Vegetarian	Jeanette Middleton	164
Remember Me	Sandi Cooper	165
The Winds of Change	Yvonne V Smith	166
See That Girl	Keith L Powell	167
A Schoolboy's Opinion Of Numeracy	Jeff Goodwin	168
Feelings	D Davies	169
The Taxi	Phillip Walters	170
In The Blink Of An Eye	Hannah Inglis	171
Tiny The Tortoise	Sadie-Louise Berry	172
Goodnight Sweetheart	Pamela Porter	173
Misery	H E Hanson	174
Missing You	Roger Stevens	175
The Stillness Of Grace	I T Hoggan	176
Big Kids On Kids	Linda Berry	177
The High Chair	Dottie Bond	178
The 'Gift' To The World	Christine Anne Davies	180
House Buyer's Lament	F Pelton	181

20 20 20 SOMETHING VISION

We oldies are golden, you can see it in our face
We have so much to offer to the struggling human race
Look beyond the creases and the colour of our hair
A wealth of life's experiences makes us wise beyond compare
We have learned such things as patience, tact and good advice
Our eye is trained to beauty and the finer things of life
See behind the wrinkles and the bones that bend with years
Life's joys and all its sorrows have sourced so many tears
We have overcome our problems, fellow travellers with strife
But the essence of our being is a wondrous love of life
I will tell the young a secret that they'll only really learn
When they are grey and wrinkly as time deems it is their turn
This life is like a painting that comes in little bits
But it's only when one's old that all the pieces fit

R Gibson

THE SONG

Call of caves and wind-whipped roar
Mist and crag and Celtic claw
White above and black below
Darkness darker than we know
Surging on towards the light
Sensing scenting through the night
Flooding forth from amber bed
Stroked with sun and dying red

Dusk descending
Green days ending

Run the ring and sing the song:
Dwell on dreams when day is gone.

Buried deep in blood and bone
Grave of gaunt and greenless stone
Dragging dust of timeless tread
Visions of the sleepless dead
Hollow voices hidden pain
Prowling wretched earth's refrain
Drink the warm-winged drowning day
Stretch the sail and drift away

Freely being
Slowly seeing

Run the ring and sing the song:
Dwell on dreams when day is gone.

Sorrow greets the bitter morn
Shallow sky unfurls forlorn
Lost forever let it fall
Far from feeling far from all
Touch the shadow's ebbing chill
Bleeding silent breathing still
Beating time to death's bold drum
Gone the glory let it come
Full-face flying
Fearless crying

Run the ring and sing the song:
Dwell on dreams when day is gone.

Miriam Mason

A Lifetime's Hobby

The old man on his allotment
Sitting on the veranda of his pigeon cree
With strained eyes, he watches the skies
For the return of his birds from across the sea.

Each time there's the same quiet excitement
Though he's flown pigeons from being a lad
And waited at the loft, time after time before that
When he was only knee high to his dad.

Then there's a dot on the skyline
Could it be? Yes, he recognises that flight
Tears prick his eyes, as his favourite blue cock
Wings its way into sight.

He rises, through a haze of Golden Virginia
And rattles the corn tin he has in his hand
Eagerly waiting, soothingly speaking
Willing the bird to land.

Now comes the time of his training
The bird swoops and drops into the loft
He puts down the tin, and quietly goes in
And within seconds has it clocked.

It's now he has that special feeling
For he knows he's bred one of the best
That's flown hundreds of miles to be back with his hen
And in this humble loft to rest.

In the club they talk of nowt but pigeons
But the times that fill him with the most pride
Are when he's up at his loft amongst his birds
Or looking at his trophies, from his own fireside.

E D Bowen

MY DAUGHTER AT LAMORNA

I remember, I remember visiting Lamorna
I parked my little brown Mini safely in a sheltered corner;
I donned my wellies, Barber, hat and issued out to gaze
Upon that wild October sea spite gale and salty haze
The sea lashed at the harbour wall, clouds raced across the sky
Gulls were crying mournfully, surely none so alone as I.
In contemplation I was lost (nearly in body too)
For that wave came out of nowhere and soaked me through
                                                  and through.
Someone called from against the wall - it was a fisherman
'When you hear that sound my handsome you don't stand there,
                                                        you run!'

Isabel (Liz) Samwells

POLTESCO VALE

Today the factory's silent
its job just here is done
no more the winch is turning
its usefulness has run

The Serpentine, once valued
and worked with loving hands
into a myriad of treasures
and sent to foreign lands

With gneiss, its neighbour, scattered
it now lies carelessly
caressed to deeper colours
by the fingers of the sea

And seabirds circling noisily
and nesting on the site
will bring up merry little chicks
where men worked day and night

Where ivy clings so lovingly
to ancient rock built wall
and looking down, sighs for the days
more lively for them all

And yet it is not gone - it's here,
for those with eyes set free,
the old Winch House is standing
waving grasses at the sea

The rocks around guard jealously
the ruins of man's hope
and gently laugh at visitors
as round about they mope

For tho the factory's silent
the men with skills long gone
as long as we remember
their spirit will live on

So let us all pledge we will keep
these Cornishmen alive
and visit - so that Poltesco
will never die - but thrive.

Nicolette A Bodilly

GUILT

A black thorn grows within,
A remainder of sin,
Once done but not again
In the scarred sheets I lay.

But still it grows more,
No vein pure
From darkened blood,
No longer good.

Claire Willis

IS THERE HOPE?

Sometimes I feel this dull nagging pain
I realise my right arm is bare
The person I love is no longer there
Here comes the pain again
Reality sets in, when can I see you?
Tomorrow seems so far away.
Will it really be there for us to share?
Promise me you will be there again.
Why does farewell have to hurt so?
Sometimes I feel this dull nagging pain.

Kevin Dixon

SCARBOROUGH

I live in Yorkshire,
It's the best place to be,
My favourite place is beside the sea,
At Scarborough.
Scarborough is the best,
So be my guest,
And why don't you
Sample it too?
An invitation,
From me to you.

Hannah E Finnegan

STEEL GIANTS

Steel giants, webbed arm
Stretched over town and farm

Skeleton ribbed, concrete feet
Anchored firm to soil and peat

Ever-ending cables, wiry veins
Transfer electricity from the mains

Silent, motionless, time standing still
Towering over tree and hill

To my eye you are invisible and yet no camouflage
Pylon with your static cargo, ever, ever charge.

Maureen Gilbert

MY THOUGHTS

As I walk along this country lane
And breathe the air and feel the rain,
I think of people who have no homes
And some no country even to call their own,
Of their terror, poverty and sorrow,
And for them, not much better tomorrow.
It really makes me wonder is anyone aware
And what is more, does anyone really care?
Aid is not the answer to everything
And nature is not all to blame,
It's the greed, corruption and dishonesty
Which are all as much to blame.
Will there ever be a time again
When man is not afraid of man,
When everything you have is yours
To keep or share it where you can?
Our children are being abused,
Our homes and shops are robbed,
The police are feeling a bit useless,
There are not enough for the job.
Our world is slowly being torn apart
And to stop it we don't know where to start.
Maybe a higher and mightier hand
Is needed to help us save our land,
So if we try a few more prayers,
Have faith and trust in God,
Then maybe we will find our way
And with God's help, manage to do the job.

M G Clements

IS IT TIME?

More often now I am feeling ill.
More often now I take an extra pill.
The old body has been through the mill.
The old body has had its fill.
The energy output is less than nil,
Sometimes my feeling is almost surreal,
I'm beginning to become like poor old Jack and Jill.
I'm beginning to struggle when going up that hill.
Maybe it's time to pay up my final bill,
Put pen to paper and write out that will.
Old Father Time is coming in for the kill,
Perhaps it's time to rest quietly and wait, nice and still,
Until . . .

David Sim

COPPED

My weekly pension I did collect
From the post office on Monday morning,
How did I know they'd given me a dud?
A twenty-pounder, given without warning.

Down to the bank I sauntered then,
And innocently passed the thing,
Suspicion was cast upon me at once,
Was the cashier going to sing?

I didn't realise, I never thought,
What consequences were about to explode,
I'd been lumbered you see and I wanted rid
So to the supermarket I went to unload.

Later that day I had a visit
From the police, well, I had been rumbled.
They talked of 'arrest' and 'deceiving with intent'
My excuses came out all sort of humbled.

'We'll sort it tomorrow,' they said quite sternly,
Making me feel like a fool.
'You'll have to pay this money back
You know, that will be the rule.'

I fretted and worried, paced up and down,
Wondering what prison term I'd serve.
Then the coppers came back with good news I must say,
'Don't do it again,' they said, 'just behave.'

'I won't! I won't!' I cried aloud,
'I'll not do it no more.'
'You'd better not,' the sarge replied,
'Or you'll be run in by the law.'

Jean Naseby

BULLIES

Bullies like to be in charge,
They can be small or very large.
They make you always feel afraid,
Their rules have to always be obeyed.

Bullies like to bend the rules,
They're around in all the schools.
Whatever they want, they think they can take,
They scheme and plan from the minute they awake.

Bullies like to cause a lot of pain,
They like to hurt again and again,
If they want something, they punch or smack,
They push or pull or give you a crack.

Bullies need to be stopped on sight,
They need to be told without a fight,
Don't give in to their demands,
Fight with *words* not with *hands*.

Ruth Sayada

A Childhood Dream

I've longed to be a poet since I was a child,
To be able to put words in verse like Burns or Oscar Wilde

Although I've wandered lonely many times,
I cannot think of any rhymes.

And it is plain for all to see,
I didn't write 'The Isle Of Inesfree.'

For I'm no William Wordsworth, a Tennyson I am not.
I'll always be the poet that people soon forgot.

Now this attempt is over, it's been a big mistake,
For I know in my heart I'm not a William Blake.

L Cliffe

The Trout Fishing Challenge

I have to write a rhyme on fishing for trout,
But this is a subject I know nothing about.
Do you use a net or a rod and line,
Or, I've heard people say, a tickle works fine?

How do you know what to use as bait,
To lure the poor things to their deadly fate?
I've heard some use maggots or maybe a fly,
But how do you know which bit to tie?

How do you know which are the trout -
Are they thin with spots, or plain and stout?
And why don't they swim in the other direction
When food looks suspicious on closer inspection?

It seems like a boring hobby to me,
Sitting all day in the shade of a tree,
Waiting for the poor little fish to bite
And how do you cope if they put up a fight?

You see anglers out in sunshine or rain,
I don't understand it - they must be insane.
Can you answer the question, 'Which are the dafter,
Those doing the fishing or the fish that they're after?'

K E Evans

A Sudden Storm

With sudden gust
The wind blew,
With forceful thrust
The storm grew.

With rhythmic drumming
The rain fell,
With ceaseless strumming
Around the dell.

With uncanny ease
The wind dropped,
With gentle breeze
The rain stopped.

With strange silence
The wood was still,
With no more violence
Save a slight chill.

With increasing heat
The sun came out,
With hearty beat,
The birds flew about.

Eddie Main

S A D

Trees are bare
Sun never shines
Tired and irritable
The usual signs

Dark mornings
Darker at night
Work in between
Pile of s**te

Too exhausted
For anything taxing
Stuff the e-mails
All that faxing

Difficult now
To muster a smile
Colleagues are worried
Can see from a mile

Getting worse
As winter comes on
Mind is lead
Happiness gone.

Steve Urwin

THE RIVER WYE

The River Wye flows sweetly on,
Regardless of the years now gone,
Of rowing eights and coxless pairs,
How I remember all the cheers.
And yet I still see fishermen,
Who can enjoy the quiet repose
Of waiting while the river flows,
Time passes by and quickly goes,
But since the battles all are won,
The river flowing quietly by,
Brings happiness that will not die.

Mary Hughes

LIFE'S PATTERN

Life is like a pattern
Made of pieces large and small
Joy and tears and happiness
It must include them all

The pattern always varies
No two are quite the same
We hope there'll be more brightness
And not much grief and pain

We only have one life to lead
To live it as we may
We don't know what the future holds
And must face it day by day

And when our span comes to its end
Our heart will cease to beat
The finished picture will unfold
Our pattern is complete.

May Morrott

LILITH FAY, DAUGHTER OF THE MOON

You came like a pale, candle flame,
Fay daughter of the moon
With diaphanous drapes shifting,
Gliding across the sea-green lagoon.
You rode the mists, you, my lovely Lilith,
Kissed by the moon's silver light,
Unfettered by the consistent land,
Your proud head thrust majestically.
Billowing winged sails
By the gentle breeze assailed.
You, sky and sea as one,
Time and tide flowing on,
Pricks of light, crystal bright,
Diamond stars blazing
And the full moon
Riding the heavens above.
You, sailing into the harbour, Lilith,
Within you, you carried my heart,
My returning love, Lilith,
So many months apart.
You cresting the frothing foam,
Bewitching galleon
Long bound from the Orient,
At last returned home
With my beloved, captain and husband, Lilith.
And tonight, as you rest in the harbour,
Me, in my bedchamber, savouring the night,
Still awake, but not alone.

Jonathan Pegg

MARINA

My eyes have seen bright temple gold
And trees with blooms I long to hold,
But there's a happy glow to see
Of friendship, full and flowing free
And Marina holds the key!

All sounds of sweetness don't compare
Or fragrance moving in the air,
With gentleness of beauty's voice
That's reached my heart, with great rejoice
In those moments pure to share.

So pleasant are Marina's ways
Fulfilment blooms from just a gaze,
Then wonder touches me anew
And I'm a cloud within the blue,
Still so light on dreamy days.

Marina's smile my heart keeps near
To last through life, forever clear,
For she's the warmth that gives delight
More than the sun at summer height,
To cherish and endear!

Peter James O'Rourke

ON STAGE

We strut like actors on a stage
We wave our arms and shout
We read our lines, page after page
But what's it all about?

This play for which we practice
This stage on which we prance
Is just for one performance
We don't have a second chance.

We make mistakes, that's certain
But we proceed to learn
We can't go back to try again
To have another turn.

For each of us the stage is set
We all must play our part
Some of us are good at it
Some play it without heart.

We've no time to do rehearsals
And if we miss our cue
We have to learn to improvise
In what we say and do.

There's no one there to prompt us
To help us do it right
We have to help each other
Till our exit - our last night.

Until the play is finished
We all must carry on
And when the final curtain falls
Let's hope they'll say - *well done!*

Lydia Barnett

LIFE

Life can be hard and cruel - or kind,
Depends part on man, and on his mind,
And part on his god, if one there be,
And if no god, then destiny.
Man paces a maze with no way out,
Yet some are sure beyond all doubt
That they have the way, know where to go -
Minds closed to truth smaller grow.
As smaller they grow, their horizons too,
Till soon the horizon's no distant view
But the boundary maze that was always there,
Viewed now with closed mind - hope, or despair?

Douglas Bryan Kennett

The Market Square Dance

I wandered afar in the summer night
An exercise of pure delight,
Halting awhile at each licensed bar,
Embracing the friendliness of the jar.
Then homeward bound, the evening spent,
Heavy of foot, but lightly content,
Soon in the sight of the market square
I felt obliged to rest me there,
Close to the man adjusting his sock,
I sat beneath the town hall clock.
It was a magical time of night,
So still - no other soul in sight.
With half-closed eyes I rested more,
Now lulled it seemed by a musical score.
The music came from I know not where;
A catchy tune that filled the air,
It inspired the feet to trip and prance,
Slowly at first, like a Zorba dance.
The increasing tempo of the beat
Aroused the sock man from his seat.
He rose to his feet and looked around,
Now captivated by the sound.
A pirouette, a ballet stance,
One hand held high he joined the dance.
He turned and swayed quiet daintily,
Matching his mood to the melody.
Now down on his haunches, his foot outflung,
Then rising, advancing, as the music swung
Into quicker tempo, a louder beat,
He tripped around so light on his feet.
Now faster and faster to the music's pace
He twirled and swayed, so full of grace,
Twisting and turning, stepping fast,
Head held high; and then at last,

He flipped a somersault and with a lurch
He landed serenely back on his perch,
Awakened by the chill night air
I treasure the sight I witnessed there.

Stan Coombs

An Ill Wind

Sometimes I get worried
On a rough, windy day,
In case my washing
Should get blown away.

Will I rush in pursuit
Claiming ownership
Of such a motley collection?
Unlikely I think!

Those items of underwear
That might have seen better days,
Usually hung out of sight
Away from curious gaze.

Old clothes I have hoarded
In case they may have use,
From multicoloured tank-tops
To barndoor-wide, flared loons.

Perhaps, far in the future,
There will be a 'Time Team'
Who will discover these relics
And wonder, who on Earth I had been!

Christine Campbell

THE BARGAIN HUNTER

School run over, 9:15,
Off to the market,
Shopping queen.
Search for a bargain,
Three for a pound -
But two-for-one's the best I've found.

To the veg stall,
Hear them shout -
'Fresh today, Missus - what d'you think about . . ?'

I look across to see the goods,
A bunch of bananas and a bag of spuds,
But my eyes are drawn to diamond studs!

The jeweller's window's hypnotic glare
Caught my attention and made me stare.
Those diamond studs were made for me -
Forget those spuds we need for tea!

I imagined myself through the window's reflection,
Earlobes sparkling, flushed complexion
And everyone would say, 'Ooh, they're so nice,'
Until finally I happen to notice the price.

Oh, cor blimey,
Oh, dear Lord,
That's a price I can't afford!
I only came to get veg for dinner,
At that price I'd have to be a lottery winner!

Back to Earth with a bump
Feet on the ground,
I go back to searching for three for a pound!

Tracey Ibbotson

AGRICULTURAL HERITAGE

I stand and lean on a metal gate,
all I survey and hear - I hate.
When did it begin? Can't remember the date.

Fields I walked as a boy and lad,
following in footsteps of my dad.
All the dreams that I once had.

All my skills built over years,
lead me to these words and tears.
How do I acknowledge all my fears?

Watching men with hedging and ditching,
how I remember my fingers itching.
Countless bales I recall pitching.

I could see the seasons change then,
watch the foxes run to their den.
Grizzled, tired, sack-shouldered men.

Now I watch the combine come,
rattling and with steady hum.
What's my life - is this the sum?

My great-grandson talks with pride,
all this machinery by his side.
To the future he will ride.

Cherry Thacker

THEY

They want you to be a couple
They want you to be a pair
You really must come to dinner
And you'll meet someone there

They want to fix you up
And come to a cocktail party
He reads books just like you
And he's just a little arty

Let's go out for the day
We know a quaint little bar
We'll meet so and so down there
And you can come home in his car

But I've been there and done that
And I know it's not for me
I've tried it all before
With husbands one, two and three!

Christine DuPlessis

NEW FOREST HUSH

Boxing day morning for breakfast and games,
A bar lunch with laughter and smiles.
A walk in the afternoon's crisp lemon sunshine,
To while away hours and miles.

Timeless nature's cathedral, space, peace and calm,
Through England's forest, kings, ponies and deer.
The place of the ancients, the home of the mystic,
Why call it 'New', when all history's here?

The colours abound as the afternoon deepens,
Greens, browns, orange, gold, surround and enthral.
The pine needle carpet, silences footsteps
As gently and slowly, the snow starts to fall.

Each different snowflake, a diamond of pattern,
The white shroud settles, a carpet of frost
Visible just, as the air slowly freezes,
A line of wild ponies, from a time almost lost.

They plod their way slowly, heads bowed in reverence,
As we watch, not moving, the last of their kind.
A moment to treasure, when back in life's turmoil,
To recall muffled footsteps, like ghosts in our mind.

Later, surrounded by log fire and laughter,
The singing of carols, and alcohol's rush.
Once in a lifetime, a privilege remembered,
An afternoon's walk in the New Forest hush.

R Ansell

FAMINE

Take a look into those soulful eyes,
then realise how lucky you are,
for that child was born into famine,
his hopes reaching wide and far.

There isn't much that he asks for,
you won't hear him moan or complain,
he just takes whatever he can,
from his desolate, dusty plain.

His empty stomach is yearning,
but he'll just have to wait,
how can there still be hunger today?
Our world's in an awful state.

He has known nothing but poverty,
has seen nothing but death,
this poor boy doesn't stand a chance,
he's just waiting to draw his last breath.

Michelle Rae

GRAVE EXPERIENCE AT ST EDBURG'S

There's a party in the churchyard, olden Hallow's Eve
A clicking celebration beneath skeletal trees
Band of coffin bearers undertake a song
A ballad first of headstone never very long

Shrouds worn as a fancy, black a perfect must
Only decoration being grey designer dust
Master of the revels, tricked out in vicar's vest
Plays violin on Earthly shin with no sign of distress

Cadavers prance in shadows, dry-iced, sightless gaze
Rapping skinless fingers on chested lids that raise
Skulls that now are empty, call upon dark moon
Tongues emerge to choral, neighbours in a swoon

Featureless the music, soulless in its beat
Tendency to disco; a wallflower's padded seat
Distantly an owl coughs, suffering diesel fume
Feathers her emotion to rock and rolling tune

Caterwaul bravado's excluded from an inn
Join the fearful dirges, exclaiming from within
Rattle raises hound dogs in Bicester's new arcade
A backdrop howl in unison, night long serenade

A skeleton existence is not a one to fear
Tumbrels bearing corpses dancing once a year
Troubadours sing beerily across our vast estate
Wine of life self-evident, joy to contemplate

Shortened life experience, soon to be engraved
Epitaph forthcoming, roaded hell that's paved
Hallows beckon yearly, bony and consumed
Fun can now be nourished, even from the tomb.

Kenneth John Webb

THE ALTERNATIVE

It is quite hard, this 'getting old':
My neck is sore, my feet are cold
And when I hear my knee bones creak,
I'm feeling like a human freak.

My eyes grow dim and slow my walk,
I start to stammer when I talk.
I used to hear 'the green grass grow'
Alas! This is no longer so.

My memory used to be fantastic,
But is no longer so elastic.
Events that did not worry me
Seem like a nightmare now to me.

At night in bed to flee the pain
I toss and look for sleep in vain,
And when I wake, start getting busy
I stumble, for I'm feeling dizzy.

As life was really not much fun
I thought, I'll ask my doctor son.
When smiling kindly I was told:
'There is one way: not getting old!'

Gertrude Black

A New Day - A New Life

The skirt she wore wasn't quite right,
At a certain angle you could see light.
Time to get new - rid of the old
She couldn't remember being so bold
Now on her own she had to change
Nothing would ever be the same
Her thoughts wandering, feeling low
She lifted her head, it was time to go.
No looking back, a new woman she'd be
Now that she was free.
He didn't love her enough to stay
Although she begged him on that day
He packed, left, without goodbye
Her heart broken, she cried and cried.
Never again will she love the same,
Control of her life - no one to blame.
She turned the key, opened the door
A new day, a new life.
Pain and tears, no more.

Ruth Newlands

HERE I AM...

My heart skips a beat with your every touch
My eyes meet with yours and I want you so much
Your lips touch mine with such softness unclear
I feel all a-tremble as I'm standing here

Your voice comes so gentle and ever so true
The way that you move me in all that you do
So touched by your presence and held by your love
Here I am standing ...

Marion McGarrigle

TONGUE-IN-CHEEK

Should thy kingdom come
Today, oh Lord
Please don't find me bored

May I be shooting fast rapids
Exploring in space
Hanging, white knuckled
From a sheer cliff face

Riding a camel
Diving for pearls
Propelled in a barrel
Over Niagara Falls

Life steeped in adventure
Fulfilling wild dreams.
I'll sing loud soprano
Till I burst at the seams

If my stamina wavers
Or age takes account
I'll heed to your calling
And gracefully bow out

Eveline Weighell

A Big Fat Ugly Day

'It is just a virus,' said the doc'
(Oh I hate his stupid face)
In fact right now I'm not too keen
On all the human race.
A stupid little virus, could not cause all this pain
It seems to me the reason is, (at least one express train
Thundering through from ear to ear
And then right back again).
'Just take the pills,' said Stupid Face
'You will be better in a week.'
Seven whole days my brain shrieks out
By then I'll be a wreck.
I struggle home and then collapse
Into my favourite chair
And think that life in general
Is really not quite fair.
So! I'll just climb up the stupid stairs
And bang the stupid bedroom door
And wallow 'neath my downy quilt
And snore and snore and snore.

Peggy Kelso

THE PENALTY KING

'It's football today, I'm going to play,'
Said Thomas, while tying his boots.
'I've been practising a lot, going to show what I've got.'
He picks up the ball and he shoots.
'Go make me proud,' Dad shouts out aloud,
As Thomas runs off up the street.
He gets to the club, legs covered in mud,
His friends, he's ready to meet.
It's raining today; he still wants to play,
Football is his number one game.
The boys play in red, one shouts, 'On my head!'
In their shirts they all look the same.
Thomas said, 'I bet, I get the ball in the net.'
He scores for his team again.
It's time for a break; they go get some cake,
They all need to dry off from the rain.
They go back outside, their boots are all tied,
They wait for the whistle to blow.
They all start to run they're having such fun,
Their faces are starting to glow.
It's coming to the end, so all of the friends,
Get ready for the penalty shoot out.
They all get in line, just one at a time,
As they shoot, all the rest shout.
Thomas gets ready to take his penalty,
Ready to kick the ball once more,
He runs at the ball, he kicks, *and he scores*
He's the penalty king today.

Haley Frisby

WE DON'T NEED PEOPLE

We don't need people
We've got PCs
Waste loads of paper
We don't need trees

We don't need to talk
We've got e-mail
We don't need the needy
The sick and the frail

We don't need to touch
We've all got our own
Faxes, scanners and Internet
Texting mobile phone

But when all the power fails
What then will we do
When you can't find me
And I can't find you?

Julie Currell

THE LOVE GODDESS

Love goddesses are created, whilst other girls are just made
and the majority just get by, in the Girlie Parade.
I suppose that there are many, that have just what it takes,
but some have an aura enamoured in the sexiness stakes!
Now one of these, not sent out on any old rally
was given the fancy name of Sally!
Specially designed up there in Heaven,
and standing all of five-foot seven . . .
Encompassed in excellence, to convey sheer passion,
her body was beautifully shaped, in such delicate fashion!
There was a softness in her voice, that would send a shudder
                                                            up your spine,
and she had that gentlest of touch, leaving a feeling so sublime!
To then, take a look into those green-blue eyes,
it seemed your were transported, straight off to Paradise . . .
She conveyed an essence of pure desire, leaving you breathless,
                                                            heart on fire!
This goddess, this gal named Sal, what more could any man require?
Like a full-bodied wine, you would drink in gentle sips,
and then that wonderful moment, when you felt the warmth of her lips.
Oh, this beautiful goddess, sent down from above,
if only 'twas me, should would give of all her love . . .
But reality had told me, that this just could not be,
for she was meant for someone else, someone other than me . . .
The Lord had planned it that way, up there in the sky,
leaving a fool like me to dream and just to wonder why?
Being in touch with her for all of 25 years,
I wonder how many heartaches there were and just how many tears?
This goddess and this actress, who had completely captured my heart,
she had gone and gotten married and my world, just fell apart!

John Franks

MY CITY

Oh my Liverpool I love it through and through,
If you're at a loss there's plenty you can do.

We have a couple of cathedrals and a big museum.
Have you ever been?

We have Beatle City and The Albert Dock,
Also the Liver Building and it has a massive clock.

There is also the pier head where you watch the ships go by
And oh my dear Liverpool, I will never say goodbye.

We have a music festival in the summertime.
It's no worse than other cities for its rate of crime.

The people are so friendly although a few are bad,
If you've never been to Liverpool, one day you'll wish you had.

Maureen Kimpriktzis

THE GARDEN OF MILLENNIA

Shimmering light falls over the ground,
Like a blanket of gold dust sprinkled around.
Into the fountain the droplets do fall,
Down flies the jackdaw onto the wall.

Spells spin around from the magical bird,
Alive come the fairies, his call they have heard.
Bright sparkling eyes shine down from above,
Millennia whispers some words to her dove.

He flies down so silently to the king lion below
And all of a sudden his crown gives a glow.
Out of a hole a gremel does run,
Calling his friends to join in the fun.

Faces appear in the rocks and a tree,
Millennia shouts, 'Come out you are free!'
More little fairies glad to stretch their wings,
'Thank you, Millennia,' they beautifully sing.

King Lion roars, 'Be quiet I can hear,'
When down on his head falls Millennia's tear.
Quickly silence falls once more,
Until again, the jackdaw opens his door.

A magical story it could be true,
Remember Millennia looks over you.

Sarah Johns

THAT ANGLER

Another Sunday morning dawns,
Maybe sunny, rain or storm.
Up he gets and strides around
Flask and sandwich to be found.

Long pole, basket, maggot pot,
Off he goes with a trot.
Down the path and up the hill
To the river running still.

Not a worry in the world,
As he sits with hook and pole,
Listening to the lonely lark
Up in the sky flying fast.

He sits and sits and watches float,
What's on his mind no one knows.
Hoping for a fish to bite
This is his great delight.

Late in the evening home he comes
Dragging foot and weary smile.
Anglers are they all alike
As they sit on basket tight?

Neilea Hames

CARELESS

His girlfriend's just come home from work.
Their baby's cried all day,
But now her mum can see to her
And he can get away.

He's had enough, he's going out
Away from all the noise.
He's going down the pub, he says,
To have one with the boys.

He never planned on fatherhood,
But just one careless night
Has cost him dear and landed him
In this, his sorry plight.

And now the kid is teething,
Her crying drives him mad.
It's not as though he wanted her,
He's not a caring dad.

He slams the door and makes his way
To where he'll get some peace.
A pint or two, a game of darts,
The tensions will release.

He's on the dole, he doesn't care,
He's got enough for beer.
His girlfriend's wage will keep him,
So what is there to fear?

He's reeling home. The night is clear.
He doesn't see the stars.
He's far too busy watching
The line of passing cars.

The traffic lights have turned to red,
A driver gently brakes.
He sees her handbag on the seat.
A minute's all it takes.

The door's unlocked, the silly cow!
She's just a careless slag.
It serves her right, he tells himself
While snatching up her bag.

She screams but he's already gone,
Immune to her distress.
He's won, she's lost, that's her look-out
He just could not care less.

Until, that is, he's cornered
And armlocked by a cop
Who happened to be passing
And saw the victim stop.

'Oh no!' says the policeman,
'Not you again! Well, well!
I guess you've just been pining
For your old prison cell.'

Back home his child stopped crying
The moment of his capture.
His girlfriend found another man
And lives in careless rapture.

Leita Donn

END OF THE LINE

It's Monday and it's washing day, outside it's blowing a gale.
I don't want to use the drier and the dampness it will entail,
So I brace myself against the elements - thick coat and hat are donned
I walk at an enforced angle - to warmer climes I could abscond.

My fingers are pretty numb, as I peg washing on the line.
What normally would take two pegs, this time I gave it nine!
As more clothes were placed upon it, the rotary began to spin.
Sheets were flapping and slapping and tangling -
I turned away and ran back in.

From inside I could keep an eye on this manic propelling ghost.
An angry sky, clouds flying by - Oh! What's happened to the post?
The line it just keeled over the beast it was quite still -
My washing strewn o'er the garden, would get dirty I did trill.

So I called my man! 'What can be done?' I did insist,
'Take the washing off, use the drier, and use some savvy Miss!'
'No I have an idea,' I confidently said.
'Just bend that pole back up again'
Saying, 'This won't work,' he scratched his head.

Well he really was obliging being muscly, ratty and strong.
He gave a shove and up it went, the washing rose up in a throng.
The wind it kept on gusting the base was full of rust
The pole it snapped, washing billowed like a sail
With husband holding the mast.

'I'll have to put it down,' he was braced against the elements.
'No, hold it there I can repair it, if the pipe will come out the cement.'
Well of course I couldn't remove it
I started to laugh and scorn.
Husband was being taken foot by foot across the lawn.

The washing it did engulf him, all beneath one could see were two legs.
By now he was shouting at me, popping off all around were the pegs.
I was laughing and trying to catch him but he wandered wither
                                                the wind blew
And finally he fell over, he was angry - this I knew.
So off came all the washing to rewash and to dry
The line went down the workshop
I got it back by and by.

It now stand two feet shorter, I can peg out on my knees.
Required to keep sheets off the ground - is a gentle breeze.
Now if it's at all windy, it still spins round and round.
It cracked me hard upon the head; I dived onto the ground.
But if a breeze is building or it's drizzling just a bit
I love that tumble drier, no, I'm really fond of it!

Judith Hill

Sunshine Sue

(Hello Sunshine Sue;) she wanders under
The willows, down by the stream
As butterflies flutter and cows gently dream
Children are playing under parents' watchful eyes
Aeroplanes soaring way up in the skies

The ice cream man rings out his wares
Children scurry and fix him with their stares
Their eyes all agog at lollies galore
Oh waiting and queuing is *such* a bore.

Money at the ready
The queue dwindles steady
Gill, Bob and Baby Harry too
Are all very happy, just like Sue!

Anne Haggarty (Angelena)

AGEING PEBBLES

The clouds of cotton wool go swimming by
Dancing to the samba of the waves
As a new design comes to the evening sky
They race away to hide in hidden caves

The sun blinks its eyelashes to the last
Graceful to this one remaining blush
One more final touch to the day that's passed
An artist with his water paints and brush

The ageing pebbles wear their night-time dress
Wrapped up in the blanket of the sand
Seagulls play a game of midnight chess
Or sing a song in their calypso band

Costume of the night is made complete
With shells and untidy weeds and things
While an elegant old swan parades her fleet
Her babies trail behind, as if pulled by strings

The ageing pebbles yawn and close their eyes
Huddled down beside the tidal reach
Where the finger tears of water tries
To wake them up and wash them from the beach

Like a child's nurse the mother moon looks down
Smiling from the depths of Heaven's bed
With tiny button stars pinned to her gown
A large and silver veil, above her head.

This sunset hand will conjure up a night
Throwing its garment on the sea
For to camouflage its shy and sleeping sight
From all, but the ageing pebbles, and me.

Robin E Edwards

STRANGERS IN TOWN

Who are they those strangers in town?
They come in their droves
And walk up and down,
Ice cream in their hands,
And buckets and spades,
They take over our sands.

But who are they, do you know?
From where do they come,
With their children in tow?
Dropping their litter and eating our chips,
They don't speak our language,
Foreign tongue on their lips.

But wait, where would we be if they stayed at home?
Or went elsewhere this year?
They might go abroad to Venice or Rome,
And not eat our chips or beer.
We'd soon miss them and their hard earned cash,
The town would very soon go broke,
And cost of living would rise in a flash.

Welcome you strangers whoever you are,
Keep coming and fill up the town.
Come in your hoards by train and by car,
With smiling faces, never a frown.
Our town is on loan through the summertime,
We lend it to you and your kin.
It is now that it blossoms and looks of its best,
Enjoy the entertainment from within.

Sue Cooper

OLD MAN

Old man, sitting by the window,
Just what have you seen?
Old man, tell me where your mind goes,
Just where have you been?

You watch the world from your old armchair,
See the people passing by,
You watch them go, though you don't know where,
And they never say goodbye.

Old man, sitting by the window,
Is it all a dream?
Old man, looking at the free show,
You want to change the scene.

You watch the world from high in the sky,
You watch the seasons change,
You make the rules, but you don't know why,
It's for you to rearrange.

Clive White

THE MOST IMPORTANT THINGS

No noise, no mess, no laughter
No phone calls, door knocks, shouts
No one to tend, run after
Visits now, only in short bouts.

They stride along my path now
Broad shoulders and a smile
My pride inside so intense, because
They make my life worthwhile.

Moulded new lives of their own
And done so very well.
Worked, loved and enjoyed
Togetherness, you can tell.

Their house, quiet, still, enough for them
But for me, a little incomplete
Too many things required
Before the sound of tiny feet.

Enjoy the noise, the mess the laughter
The joy each offspring brings.
Time will one day teach you
They are the most important things.

Morag Kilpatrick

A Poem Dedicated To The Wright Stuff

The Wright Stuff goes out on Channel Five
The programme's very much alive.

It is a debating programme that is true
Where you can express you points of view.

The presenters are Matthew, James and Kate
Three people you'll appreciate.

You will make many friends it is true
With the audience and the behind the scenes crew.

The topics vary from day to day
So why not come along and have your say.

Suzanne Reeves

My Norfolk

Of all the places in the world
There's nowhere like my Norfolk
With skies of blue and leafy lanes
She really is a *shiner*
Gold or jewels could not buy her
Not even all the tea in China!

E Barker

RESTLESSNESS

If the gifts we had been granted,
In the early days of man,
Had included just the one called *rest* -
Almost nothing would have began!

It's the restlessness that drives us.
It's round the corner we want to see.
What, why and where forever -
The searching never lets us free.

'There's something new, let's try it!
An improvement it's bound to be.
There must be something else out there,
I must surely go to see.'

Man dips his finger in every trough.
He pokes and pries around;
Till even nature surrenders,
And lets him have the ground.

It seems all other animals
Accept the status quo
Only man keeps fishing around,
To find a better way to go!

I'm grateful that it is so,
The improvements are just fine.
But, sometimes when I watch the cat
I wish her simple rest was mine!

J M Jones

My Old Garden Shed

Strange as it seems there is much to be said
About my weathered old garden shed
It's only six-foot long and four-foot wide
But you'll be amazed at what's crammed inside.

The tiny window lets in a dingy light
Enough to see a bewildering sight
Stacks of pots from plants long dead
The broom with few bristles and a loose head

A folding chair with its canvas torn
The inflatable ball impaled on a thorn
Hanging baskets I'd forgotten I'd got
With a tangle of cobwebs over the lot.

Side by side stand the spade and fork
The tales they would tell if they could talk
Be they planting shrubs or digging for spuds
These tools feel at home in our mixture of muds

There's the old push mower with blunted blades
Never again to trim shady glades
Alongside hangs a bright orange new-mo
Untangle its lead and I'm sure it will go

A perished and incontinent hose
Lies all loosely coiled in repose
No longer to be entrusted with water
Duties handed to a green plastic daughter

A dusty old hutch stands on its side
And been like that since the pet rabbit died
It was sad at the time and the children wept
So much so that the hutch was kept

Now they in turn have children of their own
The toys in the shed witnessed how they'd grown
Why the shed's filled is no longer a mystery
It's just stocked up with a family's history.

Derek Harvey

WHO CARES?

Who cares about you, who cares about me,
Who cares about people who cannot see?

Who cares about money, who cares about life,
Who cares for the girl who might be my wife?
Who cares about music, who cares about fame,
Who cares about people who call out my name?

Who cares about women, who cares about men,
Who cares what they do where, how or when?

Who cares about me?

Who cares about you?
Give me a chance and you'll see that I do.

Keith Vaughan

WATCHFUL EYE

Starlight at night
Watching, watching,
Over me,
Like a guardian angel.

The sky at night,
Is like a shroud of delight
That keeps us warm
In the cool of nuclear desertion.

The moon shines bright
In all its glory
Like *God* so glorious
With a watchful eye
Through day and night.

Leona McNicholl

HARRIET'S NEW HOME

We've a new home in Llandudno,
I don't know why we've come
But I like it in Llandudno
New homes can be fun.
Our slide is in the garden,
I wonder how that got here,
It's come all the way from Brymbo,
Is Brymbo very near?
We've both got brand-new tricycles
But I'm not very impressed,
They are shiny and bright and colourful
But I like my old car best.
We've a brand-new easel and crayons,
They taste good, honest they do,
I'll have a bit of a scribble,
Then I'll have a bit of a chew.
It's good out on our new road,
There's children everywhere,
When nobody is looking,
I'll toddle off over there.
Too late, I've been spotted,
And quickly brought in line,
Time for bed says Mummy,
No! I'm having such a good time.
I'm sure when I'm a bit older,
When I've grown an inch or two,
I'll play out with the children,
All the long summer through.
Until then I'll make do with the garden,
Lucy can play with me,
We will run and jump and be noisy,
And have picnic treats for tea.

To me everything's an adventure,
For my new home there's lots to be said,
I like it so much at the moment,
Believe me I don't need my bed.

Frances Roberts

SUNSET

Over the treetops
A cloud camel rode
With a lip-curling sneer
And a look down its nose

Then as the sky faded
From charcoal to rose
It picked up its hooves
And off it tiptoed.

Elizabeth Maria Rait

TO A WOMAN GROWING OLDER
(An old age serene and bright and lovely as a Lapland night -
Walter Savage Landor)

Old age is not a period of life
to be endured, or even much defied.
Not an enemy to slash with the knife
of forced activity, or painful pride.

Oh no. If you will accept and slow down,
the years leading to a Lapland night
are buoyant pools in which you cannot drown.
A time to notice all things small and bright.

Attractive now to young and old, you'll dress
in colours which accentuate good looks,
forever freed from that vain foolishness
which made you want to cling to fashion's hooks.

> Then in the lovely Lapland night your soul
> will gather past and present to a whole.

Margaret Munro Gibson

EXPIRY DATE

When I get up each morning,
I tend to stand and stare
Into the bathroom mirror
To see if I'm still there!
Another long night is over
A new day has begun,
I wonder what's in store for me
Before the day is done.
For when you're getting older
And running out of time,
You have to make the most of life
To waste it is a crime.
So I try not to feel self pity,
Thinking of the things that I can't do
And look around for something
That I can try that's new.
Then when evening comes round again
And it's time for me to retire
I will have done something useful
Before I finally expire!

Joyce Evans

PALMS AND BURNT ASHES

Palms and burnt ashes, with tears by the grave
Sombre sad faces, for here lies the brave
A life severed short, cut like a knife
Blood stains the white eyes, the end of a life
Wet grass and roses, cards with no scent
Black hats are bowing, crippled and bent
Rain shower sunshine soaks the green baize
Life is like death in so many ways
A spade full of dirt, the mud on the shoes
The ash-coloured coffin his widow did choose
People walk slowly, past rhododendrons in bloom
A cassette player playing his favourite tune
The hymns and the prayers, the mist of a breath
The words that are spoken all talk of death
Cucumber sandwiches with brandy on ice
Polite conversation that's ever so nice
Smiling and laughter of memories shared
Everyone loved him but nobody cared
A date for your diary, remember this day
Of the now dear departed, under six feet of clay.

Russell Phillips

FRIENDS

We loved to talk, to joke and smile
We got on together for quite a while.
I loved your smile, your cheery way
It got me through another day.
I'd wake up in the morning feeling really great
Down the stairs, kettle on, waiting for my mate.

But feelings change as days go by
I often sit and wonder why
I loved you so, you didn't know
I had to go and tell you so.
You broke my heart, you didn't care
No love for me was ever there.

Alone again what can I do?
I'm still in love with the same old you.
You often phone to say hello
But love for me will never grow.
You want a friend but not a lover
So we'll be friends for ever and ever.

Sandra Hughes

AN UNSEEN FRIEND

By the flowing stream at the garden's end full of mystery
                                            is a magical place.
There in the sun an unseen friend plays leaving no trace.

Under the moon they sing and dance, in the miniature glade
                                              they feast.
On odd occasions they rarely chance a magical meeting with me.

All alone I wait for a voice carried on a gentle breeze.
I wait for those I know exist to come and talk to me.

Victoria Louise Man

SURPRISE VIEW

We took a ride into the country up to the Hambleton Hills,
to look upon the beauty there, old cottages, lakes and mills.
As I gazed upon such scenery I wondered how long it took,
to colour this work of art like any painting book.
The patchwork quilt of many blends
with fields and hedges that never end.
Cottages nestled in the trees,
with smoke blowing up into the breeze.
Sheep, cows and hens all happy there
knowing they could have a share,
of this beauty all around.
You couldn't find this in any town!
Then as we rounded another bend
what a scene was waiting there
'Surprise View' met us with delight,
a heart-stopping moment met our sight.
Hills and vales, valleys and dells
so wonderful you could even smell
the flowers there.
Buttercups, daisies, primroses all in their own lovely way
telling us of their delight in having us there that day.
May I return again, if only in my dreams
to live again the beauty of that wondrous scene
and as I sit at home I'll say,
'Thank you for giving me that day.'

Dorothy Brown

THE STAR

Twinkle, twinkle star most high,
I'm glad the night is almost nigh.
From where you shine - to worlds do peek
And safely guard loved ones while they sleep.
Protecting them from harm and foe,
While showing them that love can grow.
Sometimes hidden by a sheet of cloud,
Or lightning which makes noise aloud.
On frosty nights your sky is clear,
Leaving icy coverings ever sheer.
To glisten under a cover, but hark
Where footsteps leave their evident mark.
Your family cradles the mighty Bear,
Just part of constellations suspended there.
Sometimes viewed by a 'scope so true,
Showing light-years that hide from the naked view.
For still you'll return for another night.
Giving travellers a safe and welcoming light.
And when the day begins to break,
Your light, of sleep it doeth partake.
To pronounce your radiance of light to burn;
Again to shine when the tides do turn.
The reason your power of which I sought,
To reach for the heart of collective thought.

Dareni

DOON AT ROSSAY FAIR

Waves of excitement filled the air
Maw says she'll take us a' tae the fair
'Noo haud yer wheesht,' said Da, 'Settle doon
And ah'll gie yeas yer fairin', a whole hauf a croon.'

We gied him a hug an' danced roon in delight
Then started tae plan what we'd buy that night
As we trailed oot the door we heard him call,
'Noo don't spend it a' at the same stall!

Keep close the gither, haud tight tae yer cash
An dinna bring back a load o' auld trash!
Ah'll meet yeas efter doon at the shows'
And we a' knew that 'efter' meant efter pubs close.

'Ahm fer the Big Dipper,' says Peter tae Ross,
'An ah might buy a hot dog wi' loads o' red sauce.'
Maw cries, 'You be careful, haud tight tae the chain,
If you break your neck, ah'll no bring ye again.'

We Tam wants a gun like they had in the war
And a goldfish that swims roon a glass jeely jaur.
Ross bought three darts tae throw on a card
He's practised a' week so it won't be too hard.

But ah' look fer artistic displays on the stalls
'Cause noo that ah'm twelve, a've nae time fer dolls.
Ah admire the fine paintings, and the earthenware jugs
How ma granny wid love they twa wally dugs.

Maw says if it rains, we'll sit in the shelter
She's worried o'r somethin' the Spey wife telt her.
Noo ah might buy ice cream, or pink candyfloss
Tam keeps asking the showfolk, 'How much does that cos'?'

Ah looked fer some pennies tae roll doon the shoot
And the crowd had a laugh when the showman cried oot,
'If yer coin's in the square and not on the line
We'll pay out your fare, or the money's a' mine.'

'Thon stall's selling towels,' said Ross, 'Come and see
A wifie bought some an' got twa bun'les free.'
Maw shook her heid an' said, 'That'll be right
She's likely been paid tae staun there a' night.'

'Tam, make up yer mind, whit ye want fae that barra'
'A whip an a peerie, or a bow-n-arra?'
'Ah'll buy Da a moothie for he loves a wee tune
But he'll dance tae ma music if he's no here soon.'

'Ma feet are sore and ma heid's goin roon
So Jeannie! Stop swithering, just buy a balloon!'
'Buy a balloon? Naw naw nae fear
Our Peter wid burst it, like he does every year.'

Ah'll wait till ma faither comes doon am thinkin'
He's just a big softie when he's been oot drinkin'
He'll slip me some siller, tae add tae ma tips
An' on the way hame, ah'll buy us a' chips.

Jenny Brown

THE SIMPLE MAN

I have a friend a simple man
Does not fit in with life's great plan
Goes through life with a little smile
Easy to laugh, hard to rile
He knows everyone by name
Treats the good and bad the same
Always ready to lend a hand
Anywhere and time he can

Spends his time doing good
Always pleasant never rude
I've never heard him raise his voice
If he is angry it's not his choice
He'd rather turn and walk away
And speak again another day
He's not afraid it's just his way

So my friend he goes through life
Loving his children and his wife
Trying to help his fellow man
Any way he thinks he can
A simple man with simple ways
This is how he'll spend his days
His idea of happiness
A man that God will surely bless.

Allan McFadyean

A Seventeenth Wedding Anniversary

Out of the blue the date comes round
with special joys regained
and lingers long enough for both
to know it's well sustained,
with commitments to the need to work
tae feed the bairns an aa that.
It's nice tae ken - keekin back tae then,
ye've made the grade for aa that!

Andrew A Duncan

NEWSPAPER SHUT-DOWN

There's no jobs to be had in Fleet Street,
Or in the local paper offices.
No news is bad news and good news is bad news,
So there are now no press releases.
There's nothing to say, no sneak gossip,
No celebrities seen down on the ground.
All strive to be blameless and all succeed,
So not even suspicion can be found.

You'd think that the Stalins and Mugabes of this world
Had proliferated, gone out, with flags unfurled.
Business blocks to let, titles we now forget,
And paparazzi into prison hurled.
But the benevolent dictator rules. To be kind, he is cruel.
Through lack of trade, and shame, and public outrage,
Through being unnecessary and sinful smears memorably,
These houses of hypocrisy have ended their days.

A perfect world for me, an Eden dream to be
Where this streak of control freak is dead to stay.
Those manipulative minds, thought controllers, mental spies,
All disappeared forever, gone far, far away.

Then I woke up, and went to the shop
And found (though I knew) my vision was made up.
For as we love tales, we motivate their sales.
Original sin keeps this poison on its rails,
And if we didn't buy, we'd see them go.
This filth would vanish to time's passing flow.
Yet I know the perfect is some time to come.
Let's hope 'some time' is short in the long run.

Andrew Sanders

A Visit To The Bank

I went to see the bank manager today,
to enquire about a loan.
He was not in,
so I spoke with another man,
who had just put down the phone.

He listened intensely
as I explained my quest.
After some thought,
and a scribbled calculation,
he slowly shook his head.

'I am afraid it is all down
to the interest rate,
it is very high,' he said.
'And you have a job
which goes against the current trait.'

So we stood and shook hands
the way most people do, he kept on smiling all the while,
as though he knew the punchline to a joke.
I wish he had told me
I could have done with a smile.

Paul Kelly

A Book Of Poems

I have found a book of poems
that makes my heart delight
to the sweetness of these poems
I dedicate soul's sight.

I have read my deepest treasures
within these pages of gold
not one other experience measures
as the secret words unfold

Had I lived another lifetime
I could not wish to have captured
such intense and pleasured pastime
that has my soul enraptured

When limbs grow old, when love has failed
and disillusioned hearts weep
poetic words, fond memories hailed
revive hope, touch feelings deep

I have found the book of poems
all time and toil stands still
from the sweetness of these poems
parched memory takes it fill.

Edna D'Lima

BOY RACER - AN ESSEX TALE

There were skids in his pants
And skids on the road
As Boy Racer showed
No interest at all in the Highway Code.
He had it all, matey,
Halogens that glowed,
Exhaust pipe that bellowed,
Obligatory dice, furry and yellow,
And the belief that the corner
Was definitely do-able at 80.
There were skids in his pants
And skids on the road,
No one looks good under flash blue
And scrap

Jon Oyster

OLD VIENNA

I dreamt I was in old Vienna
Standing on a ballroom floor
I saw a magical scene before me
Such as I had never seen before

Everywhere was colour
Everywhere was light
The dancers on the ballroom floor
Were an absolute delight

On the balcony up above me
Stood boys in sailors' attire
In harmony they sang together
The Vienna Boys' Choir.

The orchestra played waltzes
And several polkas too
Conducted by Johann Strauss
Which thrilled me through and through

My dream suddenly faded
The magic had all gone
How I wish I could see once more
The old Vienna of Music and song.

H Willmott

STUDENT DAUGHTER

I miss her when she's gone away
No more chocolate brownies on a tray
No more teatime treats on a working day
No Victoria sponge, but that's OK -
Because I need to watch my weight
And I've felt like a lorry with a tonne of freight!

But oh she brightens up my day
She's a ray of sunshine in my way
When overhead the skies are grey
'Where's Mum? Where's Mum?' - but that's OK
Of green causes she's an ardent fan
Seeking out an eco-warrior man!
Soon end of term and then we can
Drive north to south in a hired van!

Trish Duxbury

UNTITLED

Take me to your world
Where the land is green
Where cats sit curled
And fairies have been

Take me to your home
Where it's warm and free
Where fires burn brightly
For you and for me

Take me to your waterfall
Where blue waters flow
Where fish swim free
And rainbows show

Take me to your heart
Where I can stay
Warm and tender
Like sunshine rays

Take me to your life
So I can play
So I will love you
For the rest of my days.

Bonnie Middleton

A Child's Country Dream

When I fell asleep last night,
I had a funny dream,
I was playing in the country,
Things were not what they seemed.
The builders were a-building and the road's upside down,
And lovely fields had disappeared and nowhere to be found.
As I got deeper and deeper in my dream
I heard a dreadful noise and a child began to scream,
'What are you doing? You can't dig there!'
'That's where Mummy and I come to the country fair.'
'Listen child,' a tall man said, 'you have to move with the times,
Otherwise, I wouldn't earn a dime,'
I stared in bewilderment, could not believe my eyes,
As trees were falling heavy on the roadside.
Then I tried to visualise what the fields looked like before,
But it was too difficult with the noise galore,
I remember going home and putting wrongs to right,
Telling mum and dad we must put up a fight,
To try and stop them building and losing countryside,
But all mum and dad did was give a heavy sigh.
'Now child you're too young to be bothering about such things,
You have to change with the times, so do not make such a din.'
And deeper and deeper I went into my sleep, I did not like this dream,
Then all of a sudden I stepped and was looking on
At the dream I was having, such a distressing one.
Perhaps it was just a message or a simple sign for me
That I would be campaigner for the countryside constantly,
And as a campaigner and people on my side,
My early dreams would then come alive.

Carol Boneham

WHAT DID I DO?

What did I do
To desire this
Stress and aggro?
If I had one single wish
I'd go back to start again
And tell you it was wrong
Why won't you listen?
Can't you see?
There's going to be trouble
And grief
And you'll be in the middle
You always are
And always will be.
You think you're hard
But the things you do
Are stupid and silly
But will you listen?
No!
You need to stop fooling yourself
You're not as hard as you look
Just remember that next time
When you do something like you did
Ask yourself
Why me?
Why was I there?
Then perhaps you'll remember that breaking up your family
Isn't worth it just to act hard and look cool.
That's all I want to know
What have I done to you?
To go through this now and feel as guilty as you.

Laura Perkins

AIN'T LIFE A BITCH!

It seems to me that life's a bitch
From nappy rash to the seven year itch
From mis-spent youth and that first kiss
To spotty faced teens then wedded bliss

From motherhood to reaching 30
To memories of 'weekends dirty'
Approaching 40 - ain't life a drag
Wrinkles appear and flab starts to sag

40 becomes 50 with hair turning grey
Varicose veins from standing all day
All too soon it's 60 with arthritic knees
Embarrassing moments whenever you sneeze

Just a short time away from the big *Seven-O*
Will the rest of my teeth be the next thing to go?
Will my hair now fall out - will I manage four score?
Maybe a Zimmer frame - but one thing's for sure

Ain't life a bitch or is it a breeze?
Can you turn back the clock? Well, tell me how *please!*

Pam Tucker

FIND TIME

Time, time, time, time
Never-ever find the time
All I ever seem to find
Is that I just don't find the time
So make the time
To take the time
To use and not abuse the time
So much to see
And think and do
To try to find the time for you
And whilst I worry about losing time
I find you growing all the time
So one step back
Once more, this time
I'll find the time
To find the time

James W Bull

A Visit To Howarth

We set off for Howarth, 'twas a very fine day,
The countryside decked in its summer array.
Set like a gem on a steep hillside,
A historic setting, a poet's paradise.

Cobbled streets awaited us there,
Shops filled with craft everywhere.
This famous village whence we were bound,
Boasts an ancestry, of authors renowned.

We joined in the pilgrimage,
Walked to and fro.
Absorbed the atmosphere,
Till we had to go.

As we pulled away,
With a last nostalgic look,
We recalled the pages,
Of the Brontè books.

Molly A Kean

IDEAL WEIGHT

'You're fairly putting on the weight,'
They say with obvious glee.
It's hard not to get distressed
The way folks talk to me.

They think cos you've an extra
layer of fat under the skin,
That nothing can get through to you,
No emotion can seep in.

They say things like 'My, you're getting stout.
You really have filled out!
Haven't you got big fat thighs?
Shame! cos you've got nice eyes.
But then, you've got a big chest too,
I've got a smashing diet for you.'

'No thanks,' I say 'you keep it!'
'It's really a shame!' they coo,
'Wouldn't she look smashing,
If she lost a stone or two!'

Rebecca H Weir

THANK YOU TONY BLAIR

It was supposed to help me,
Back into work,
But in a room full of strangers
I felt such a jerk.
What was I doing here?
I felt such a geek,
But this feeling wouldn't last
For more than a week,
Because I had noticed
One major thing.
He made my pulse race
And my heart sing.
By the end of the second week,
We were lovers.
We didn't find jobs,
But we did find each other.
Now we are married,
With a daughter, Sarah-Lou.
So Mr Blair,
All I can say is 'Thank you!'
You had an idea;
New Deal, Back To Work Scheme.
You also bought to life
My every dream.

Rachel Hobson

JOURNEYING FORWARD, LOOKING BACK

When all around is dim and grey
And all is lost at sea
There's often a gap in every day
When something touches me.

A twinkle in a child's face
The flutter of a wing
A chink of light around my space
Will lighten every thing.

A song will spark a memory
A perfume brings back a day
My thoughts float by reminding me
Of a brighter summer's day.

Collect each loving feeling
Count them one by one
Each blessing sends me reeling
To a brighter constant sun.

Look forward to tomorrow
Embrace it to its end
Stare in the face of sorrow
And know you have a friend.

Build a wall of pleasures
Watch it grow so tall
A wall of solid treasures
Will catch you if you fall.

Cast a spell of wonder
To whisper in the night
Put enemies asunder
Shout! And scream! And fight!

Susan Gale

TEA BREAK

We built a dam to stop the stream flowing back into the sea.
We dug deep to make a lake, my sister, my brother and me.
In the lake that we created, we floated our model ships
And we piled the sand dam higher with rocks and other bits.
We dug out docks and long canals in which our boats could sail
With spades and hands we piled up the sand - sometimes we used a pail.
The stream still flowed down the beach and filled our deepening pit
And gradually ate the dam away, bit by little bit.
So we built the dam bigger, stretched it further along the beach
But the flowing water was too strong, it suddenly caused a breach.
Oh so quickly we repaired the hole, but another one appeared
The imprisoned flow was beating us, then just as we feared
The dam collapsed, the trapped torrent rushed to meet the sea
But we were happy to let it go as Mum called us in for tea.

Mike Jackson

THE DRIVING TEST

It was the day of my first driving test
and I wanted to do my very best,
my good driving, you'd adore,
at the lesson just before.
But to the Test Centre - I was due next.

I sat in a small poky room,
awaiting my impending doom.
The door opened, a man
with clipboard in hand,
said 'Ah, you're next I presume?'

I started my driving quite well,
but the roundabout, it was just hell!
I approached it too quick,
I felt really sick,
I'd blown it, I'd failed, I could tell!

I nearly went into the side
of a car with a driver surprised
at the action I took,
because I didn't look
and I'd taken the corner too wide!

My emergency stop was okay,
at least I stopped anyway!
My three point turn was five,
how would I survive,
this terrible stressful day?

We stopped at the side of the road,
for a test on the Highway Code.
I was still feeling queasy
but his questions were easy,
and I knew all the roadsigns he showed.

He'd failed me and I felt quite sad,
but to pass me, he would've been mad!
So I would try again,
practise harder and then
I'd pass next time, that wouldn't
be so bad!

Marion Scarlett

IMAGINE

Imagine that you
Could see into the future
What it has in store for you
Imagine that the oceans
Were grey instead of blue
Imagine that the birds
No longer sing their songs
Imagine that all the trees
Have all long since gone
Imagine all the meadows
Lifeless silent and bare
Imagine all of this
Yet no one seems to care

Alan Green

A Day's Journey

You creep above the distant hills,
flaming moor and field and heath.
From tree and branch dawn's chorus fills
and stirs the sleeping world beneath.

You climb, the mists begin to fade
and crimson shafts pierce copse and hedge.
Your scattered rays streak light and shade,
pink tip the earth from edge to edge.

Shadows shorten as you climb,
higher and yet higher still.
The world below awakes to time,
the treadmill round of hours to fill.

The clouds that race across the dawn
are patchworked now with grey and red.
They rise and change to greet the morn
'til every colour trace has fled.

Your noon-tide warms the land below
and crops and cows seek sunshine's ray.
Bright sunflower heads turn as they grow,
while children dawdle, hide or play.

Too soon begins your slow descent,
the shadows lengthen from the west.
The farmer nods, 'The day's far spent.'
And bairns and birds and beasts seek rest.

Once more a fiery ball, you fall
through cherry-flavoured, slanting night.
And from the kitchen comes the call,
'Will someone, please, put on the light.'

Daphne Clarke

Working In The Coal Mine

Albert sitting in his old armchair
His breathing was painful and slow
He thought of his life when he was young
When he worked underground long ago.

Eleven years old he followed
his dad and his brothers
To work down the pit every day
The hours were long and the conditions were poor
All for very little pay.

He remembered when he was twenty
His shift was over for the day
When suddenly there was a fall of earth
He was trapped, like a rat in a cage.

It took six hours before he was rescued
The air was stale and dank
But as he was brought out on a stretcher
He looked up to the Lord and gave thanks.

Yes, the memories will always be with him
His pain will always be there
From his days underground he is suffering
As he sits in his old armchair.

Audrey Machon Grayson

LANDSCAPE

A stretch of browning yellow sand
Smooth as silk, untouched by any hand
Virgin territory, yet undefiled by feet
Where, on occasion, strangers meet.
Rocks and pools circle the groynes
That are part submerged in shifting sand.
A tongue of grass protrudes beyond
Along the jutting headland, free.
Crops harvested, crew-cut corn
Left to wait for man to burn.
Sun glistens on the sea,
Tide comes creeping to the shore,
Stones are wet, pebbles shine,
Wind is rising, clouds are forming,
Chill is coming, gulls are wheeling:
Time to go!

Muriel Hughes

Goodbye

No work have I,
No outlook on life.
For I live in the valleys,
Where unemployment's rife.
I've a family to keep,
And mouths to feed,
So trudging the roads,
Until my feet, they bleed.
Looking for work,
But to no avail,
Same old story,
Now they've closed Ebbw Vale.
More on the jobs list,
So here I cannot stay,
For I'll have to leave my family,
And go work away.

Steffen AP Lloyd

TIME

A house that used to ring with noise
Scattered clothes unwanted toys
Silent now, nothing stirs
Towels folded his and hers.

Rooms sit empty, books in rows
Time passes how it goes
Children will be coming home
Adults now how they have grown

Gone to study far away
They like it there, or so they say
We bought them drinks, coke and Fanta
I really miss my role as Santa

And when we sit around the fire
Hear them talk we never tire
Making plans to go away
We know deep down they cannot stay

So let's rejoice, we have them here
Raise our glass and drink good cheer
To have them home what ere the reason
At this special Christmas Season.

Daniel P Taggart

HAPPY TO BE

As I sit under a willow tree
I look up to the beautiful blue skies above me
Happy to be alive, to see
all the beauty that surrounds me
I feel so honoured to be part of
its life to you see
As the sun shines down
I feel it warmth around
under my feet
I'm just so happy to be
alive, healthy, happy the way I am
There's nothing more I wish for
in life you see
I have everything I want in
nature's pathway of life
forever to be.

Sharon Brown

TERRY CASEMENT

Pull up a pew
And sit down here for a few.
Terry enjoys the crack,
But just watch your back!
A story or two
Or maybe he'll tell ya who's who!
You'll be laughing, crying, singing,
And that's only the twelve bells ringing.
As the afternoon draws,
He'll know all your flaws.
He met a sweet girl called Mary,
She was his only fairy.
Eleven children she did bare,
I bet that was a handful too rare,
Although money for food was very tight,
The love he gave made everything right.
The clothes he wore were passed from relations
Probably passed down for many a generation.
Stories were told of having no shoes,
Back then they had nothing to lose.
The long stretch of brick on the Downpatrick Road,
Reminds me of his massive work load.
Morning until night, the work carried on,
A few drinks at the weekend followed by a song.
His sweet Mary has since passed on,
Heartbroken he'll carry on,
In his life he has been loving and strong.
Terry is a wonderful man,
I know, I am his number one fan.

Leigh-Ann Sloan

A Lady

To a lady, yes a lady, who has seen many things pass like a dream
A lady, nae a great lady, whose many memories of life flow
                                                                         like a stream
A lady who has turned, yes turned, many bad things into good
But a dear lady who would not swop her lifetime even if she could
A lady whose once fine head of hair may now be turning snowy white
A lady who still sheds many a silent tear for the wrongs she could
                                                                           not right
A lady who truly loves so much and often says a silent prayer
A lady who still remembers fondly, people and places no longer there
A real lady, yes, so proud to be known by people both far and wide
A lady who as time has proved, has seen the turning of many a tide
A dear lady who means oh so much and finds a place in many hearts
A lady who in her lifetime has acted in oh so many parts
A lady who when needed becomes an angel in disguise for both the
                                                                   young and old
A lady with a true heart of gold, a lady of whom many stories are
                                                                     yet untold
A lady who when the last day dawns will face the day with her
                                                                     usual smile
A lady who knows that really a lifetime in reality lasts only for a while

R Tate

UNTITLED

You know that I'm in Heaven
I just want you to know
That I am always with you Mum
And that I love you so

I'm there when you are sleeping
I'm there when you're awake
To love and protect you
Whatever it may take

I'm your little angel
I'm watching from above
To be there to guide you
And bring you so much love

You know that when in spirit
You know we never die
I'm that bright star around you
Up in the big blue sky

M Simpson

THE NEIGHBOUR

I passed by your window early today,
Old man with hair so sparse and grey.

There you sat on rickety chair,
Head in hands in deep despair.

I am sad and lonely too,
Lost my dear ones, just like you.

Poor old man, let me make you smile,
Visit you and sit awhile.

Reminisce on days gone by,
Talk a little of you and I.

I will peel you an orange
Bake you a cake or two.

After all it seems to me,
The neighbourly thing to do.

Old man you look much better now,
I really wonder why?

And could that be the glimmer,
Of a twinkle in your eye?

N V Wright

THE DAY YOU WERE BORN

I remember so well
The day you were born
Brought joy to my life
On a cold grey morn

Feeling so nervous, feeling afraid
What will I do, what will I say?
Couldn't even hold you, you're so very small
What if I drop you, what if you fall?

So very precious, my beautiful child
Just to look at you, bring tears to my eyes
Tears of joy, that make me so glad
So very proud, being your Dad

Home you came, things going to change
My life never will be the same
No more sleep, no time to shave
Baths to give, nappies to change

I sit by your bed, watching you sleep
So very beautiful, making me weep
Wanting to tell, all of the world
You're so very precious, you're my little girl

Watching you crawl, learning to walk
Seeing you smile, hearing you talk
The sound of your laugh, the feel of your tears
These things I'll remember, down through the years

When I am old
And things have changed
I'll never forget
The day that you came

A Hunter

WITHOUT HIM

The curtains fall down - what do I care?
The way I feel, they can just lie there,
Then would you believe, bulbs start to blow,
I can change a light bulb - that I know,
but . . . I find the fittings are hopeless
and I could not cope - less.

The bathroom light was the worst,
I began to feel that I was cursed,
a bath in the dark - is not the same,
I managed with light shining thru the door frame.

The shower curtains and rail go next,
now I am feeling downcast and vexed,
Light in the kitchen is so temperamental,
sometimes I feel it will drive me mental.
I did change the tube and charger,
but the problem just gets larger.

Hole appears in garage door,
rotting wood is such a bore.
Water butt now disengaged,
base foundation - having caved,
tap is broken anyway,
this I will leave for another day.

My garden table took off one windy day,
I now have a three-legged table - to my dismay,
Fence collapsing at the side,
So grateful, it is not too wide.

Washing machine gives up the ghost,
I really did miss this the most.
TV too difficult to view,
time is to replace that too.

Music Centre sent for cleaning and repair,
now tape stuck in it - life is so unfair.
New gas fire now installed
bird trapped in chimney - I was appalled.
Gas man came - bird set free
Now it's down to poor old me,
as gas fire now left disconnected
I need to get it resurrected.

Bedroom handle should be on door,
it is now in my hand - such a bore.
Double glazing is now complete
it is looking really neat,
apart from windows bare and exposed,
blinds down, who will fix? Goodness knows!
Oh I forgot about the bell
Visitors now have to bang or yell.

What prompted me to pen this rhyme,
until today I was doing fine,
then calamity struck (there is no doubt)
because today my tooth fell out!

E J Prout

Foot And Mouth Disease

An outbreak of foot and mouth disease
awakens rural fear and unease
as animal slaughter gathers pace.
Farmers, fearful of a single case,
when years of toil and devotion
will be extinguished by its embrace.

Vets struggle to contain
this scourge of cattle; a murrain.
Condemning those that are afflicted
and those who yet may be affected
through close contact, despite countrywide
access that is restricted.

Removed from all but those engaged
in slaughter, children are outraged
at their isolation and quarantine.
In frustration they stamp and scream
at the crumbling of their world.
A bloody, nightmarish dream.

Padlocked gates and chains
contradict government ministers' claims.
The countryside is open they say,
go out, enjoy your walk and play.
Support the rural economy
despite burning fields and decay.

Robert Allen

PAIN

Emotional and physical pain in the end it feels just the same.
Stabbing again and again, a constant thought in your brain.
Can your heart and body take the strain?
Smiling being nice, nothing left to gain.

Nagging and gnawing like a relentlessly speeding train.
Popping a pill, hoping the aches will be slain.
Till the hurt comes back, oh how do I stay sane?
Without my world swirling down this painful drain.

Andrew Crump

FIRELIGHT PICTURES

A lovely wide old fireplace
And pine logs crackling bright;
Oaken beams and brasses
Which gleam in flickering light.
A Toby jug whose portly face
Is smiling from a shelf,
And I'm snugly sitting in this
Room, all by myself.

Outside the snow is thickening
But in the evening gloom,
With shadows gay for company
I snuggle in this room.
Before the fire, sat on a stool,
I warmly toast my toes,
And picture in the friendly flames
Just what the old room knows.

A memory of a handsome face -
A dashing Cavalier -
Who hid inside the secret room
That's panelled somewhere here.
A Royalist man, whose rousing voice
Had made the rafters ring;
Pouring scorn upon the men
Who turned against their king.

A memory of a violin
Which played a dreamy waltz.
A girl dressed in a crinoline -
The violinist halts.
He meets the sweet girl's bright blue eyes,
A blush steals o'er her face,
And words of love were spoken here
'Midst lavender and lace.

Sweet memories of such happy times,
If sad ones came as well
The old room keeps them to itself,
And happy stays the spell.
So can you wonder why I love
To sit here by the fire,
And hear the room weave lovely tales
Of which I never tire?

J Packwood

NORMAN'S LAMENT
(Memoirs of Norman Lamont)

The pendulum is swinging slowly left and right
You see I have a problem, I am none too bright!

Saddam Hussein and Bosnia aren't helping very much,
If things don't perk up pretty soon, I'll have to ask the Dutch!

Declare a war on Bundersbank and that Chancellor Kohl,
I really must do something about this wretched mole!

The economy is failing, and so is my health,
Perhaps I'll tax the royals on their unearned wealth.

They say that I am callous, they say that I am cruel,
They say that it's beneath contempt to put a tax on fuel.

The party's over
And so I am going on my way
They say I flunked
Now there's nothing left to say.

And so I am sinking into the depths of my despair
And I am thinking, does any body care?

I have been cheated
By the very man I trust
Being mistreated
How can I earn my crust?

I used to massage figures
To satisfy my boss
He gave me the old heave-ho
Now I'm very cross

I'm very good with figures
So is 'Miss Candy Floss'
I'll offer her employment
And enjoy being her boss!

Ben Wolfe

CONSCIENCE

You chase me down the pathways of my mind,
you run in the wake I leave behind.
You tap my shoulder, turn me round,
you grasp my elbow, throw me down.

Oh sweet Conscience, now you're mine,
now your whisper is a loving kind.
Run with me for ever more,
ride with me to heaven's door.

For now I see how great you are,
you walk my feet on a golden bar.
You speak my voice so loud and clear,
you give me life, what's there to fear?

Tim Coburn

IN THE NAME OF RELIGION

The world is full of strife,
People battling for life.
We wonder where it leads,
For all the different creeds.

People talk about religion
How theirs is the only true one.
But if they all followed their profits truly
They would never be so unruly.

This one saying follow our Prophet
As ours is the only one.
Another one says follow my Saviour
As he is the only one.

But if they were truly men of peace
They would make sure violence would truly cease
Not carry on their war and call it Holy.
When destruction seems to be the only word surely,
They can see no good will come of this vision.
In the end the only losers are the innocent people
Who are killed in the name of religion.

If you believe in Mohammed, Buddha or Jesus.
Show a bit of tolerance for each other's differences.
Respect each other's right to believe
In any religion that they please.
Not force each other's opinion on the other
Treat them like you would a brother.

Until we can live together in peace
Human kind will find no release.
Until we stop cruelty and hate
People will have sealed their fate.
Until we stop this rot and ruin
I can find no hope for human beings.

Margaret P Thomas

LIFE WITHIN LIGHT

A newborn lies in his mother's arms,
Untainted and innocent, full of life's charms,
He travels life's road, achieving his goals,
Who could have predicted what his future would hold?
The dark side of life beckoned and called,
The urge was too strong - no resistance at all.
How many times had they been shown the signs?
Unconditional love had clouded their minds.
It's each parent's nightmare, could they have done more?
Deceit, lies and anger when their child had to score,
Substance abuse has scrambled his mind,
Not the child they once knew, so loving and kind.
He's travelling so fast - Angels can't keep the pace,
He's surely the winner in this lap of death's race,
We'll all say we're sorry, and gather around,
Sorrow mustn't end here, as he's laid in the ground,
Who will be next to experience the pain?
'Pray God it's not us!' will be the refrain,
We must all work together to scourge this disease,
Don't leave it to others - or the dark side we'll please.
Let our bright lights shine through for all, not select few,
For if our child gets lost, who will they turn to?
Don't you see friends, we're all part of the same family,
It's my child and yours, not others' children we see,
If we all play our part with God's grace we will be
Returned to the plan for humanity.
When the child is re-born, past life paid for in full,
The debt has been cleared - contributions from all,
Let's pray for the day when the dark side will be
No more to that child, than a memory.

Like beacons let's guide those lost through the storm,
But there have to be others to keep shining on.
For when our light's extinguished on this side of life,
Let the ones who remain, keep glowing bright,
No more darkness to tempt and torment our child's friend,
Each life bathed in light, to its natural end.

Elaine Nicholas-Chan

12:24 TO DEANSGATE

I stand on the platform
awaiting my train
clickety-clack
say the rails again.

I look up at the clock
on the station wall
clickety-clack
the final call.

Smouldering cigarettes
on the cold stone floor
clickety-clack
they sound the horn

. . . train flashes by . . . the air is torn

clickety-clack, clickety-clack, clickety-clack . . .

Heather Olly

THE GIFT

We are all given it, sometimes large and sometimes small
And if we are rich or poor
Do not waste it, or give it away
But treasure it day by day.

Make it last as long as you can
Use it to help your fellow man
The longer you have it
The smaller it grows.

When it can disappear without trace
And is impossible to replace
What is this gift more precious than gold
A treasure chest of wealth untold
The gift with all it's high and lows.

Is life of course, wonderful life.

Doreen Wilkinson

HOORAY

Around the world
In a Christmas ball,
Wickering on
Modest smile against the fall.

Seeds in the wind,
Fire in the belly,
Fast man Fossett
Is better than the telly!

Anita Layland

WARBIRD

The plane stood by the runway
Both proud and battle worn
A first class fighter in its day
Of the Second World War.

Its guns at the ready
The Merlin ready to roar
But the prop remains still
There's no need to fight any more.

I wonder what it must have been like,
To meet the enemy, eye to eye
To watch in terror as a Heinkel
Falls from the sky?

Then my trance is suddenly broken
As they swoop from above
With both speed of an eagle
And the grace of a dove.

One by one they disappear
Into the clouds and out of sight
But the plane remains by the runway
Maybe one day she'll take flight.

But for now it stands as a message
A reminder to us all
That we must remember the heroes
Who gave their lives to save us all.

Raymond Hill

I Love The Night

I love the night
Its strength and its might.
Its darkness surrounds me
As black as can be
I love the night
It's a god without light.
I love a cold frosty night
With its sharpness and bite.
I love the night
When it bursts into light
And, I love the day
When it's golden and bright.

C A Keohane-Johnson

THE FAMILY'S LAMENT

The carpet-layer came yesterday,
He seemed a real good type,
Until he managed to knock a nail
Right through the main gas pipe.
The gas man came and mended it
And said it is now all right.
So we're waiting for the carpet-layer
To come and finish the job, tonight.
He might feel quite fed up with us,
But we shall be real glad
To see the backside of him,
And stop our Mum, from going mad.
Hooray, he's done the job at last,
Poor chap! He looks quite tired,
We'll tell his boss, how good he was.
Cos, we wouldn't want to get *him* fired.

Marjorie Seaman

A True 'Storey'

Emily, Emily, somebody cries
Emily, Emily, no one replies
A mother in panic surveys the store
Granny changes direction calling more
I see their faces chill with fear
Emily, Emily no sign of her near
Frantically they search between each pile
I retrace their steps and begin to smile
I see the hide-out Emily has found
A display of cushions, a colourful mound
Suddenly a little head peeps through
I asked about something I already knew.
'Is your name Emily?' She is excited
'I'm hiding from Mammy,' oh so delighted.
She snuggles under the cushions again
Unaware that now it is all in vain
Hastily I bring Mammy to hiding place
To witness a tearful yet loving embrace
The store did not have what I sought
But oh the joy, 'just being there' brought.

Sarah Smeaton

THE LADY OF THE JAGUAR

On either side the motorway
the banks and fields in spring display
wild flowers that bloom in fine array
that catch the eye, this sunny day
when driving down to Cardiff town

She joined the M4 miles afar
in her imposing Jaguar.
She looked just like a movie star.
It is of course her father's car
she's driving on to Cardiff town

The wondrous sight her senses drown.
In the fast lane she changes down.
Annoyed behind 'Who is this clown'
His brow is furrowed in a frown.
'Who drives so slow to Cardiff town?'

He will be late, always a strain.
He blew his horn, he can't remain
at this slow speed, he shouts in vain
'You should be in the nearside lane
if going off to Cardiff town.'

She's so entranced, she's unaware.
She doesn't think though mirror's there
to look behind, she'd see his stare
of hatred for her lack of care
for others passing Cardiff town.

His foot goes down, the gears engaged.
He rams her car, he is enraged.
The car turns over at this stage.
He gave no thought for her young age.
She dies because of his road rage.

E Davies

TIME - LIFE'S PREDATOR

Time is a predator that stalks us all our lives
It rules our waking hours but when we sleep it seems to dive
Only to surface far too soon to rise us for our working day
The nights seeming far too short for it to ever go away.

Time is a companion that accompanies us on our way
It reminds us to cherish every moment come what may.
Remember that favourite place we visited so long ago?
The years have passed so quickly, is it still too late to go?

Time is the enemy that can rule our waking hours
Knowing that it's limited, can change the ruling powers
The end could be hours, days, months or even years.
The threat is always there and can never allay our fears.

Time can be your friend, with absence time can heal
Distance can be a blessing to give you space to feel
The loss of someone loved, or someone gone away
Time can help you understand where emotions have gone astray.

But time is the predator who stalks us all our lives
Follows our every footstep, never wavering as we strive
To keep our lives in harmony with friends and foe alike
When time runs out the future is decided, and that is when it strikes.

Sheila Storr

THE INJECTION

I decided this year to be incredibly brave
A flu injection's sensible, all fears I would stave
All the way there, my knees did a wobble
Then I felt sick and began to hobble
I crawled to the desk, she said 'Wait in the queue.'
I was the twentieth person, well I ask you!
They went, one by one, upright, unfeared
They came out ashen and nearly in tears
By the time I was laying in about twelfth place
I was sweating, pulsating, but keeping face
My arm ached already and I hadn't been in
I wish the man in there wouldn't make such a din
The receptionist kept giving me funny looks
'It's a new doctor,' she said 'but he's read all the books.'
Two more in front, then it's my turn
These palpitations are making me squirm
Now where's my tissue, I'm going to sneeze!
All this tension is making me wheeze
Next! Oh no, it's me now he's calling
Well here goes, oh my courage is falling
'Oh come now' he says 'don't be afraid,'
If only he knew how many times I had prayed.
'You sound a bit chesty, have you a cold?'
Oh a terrible one, another lie told.
'Well I'm sorry, no injections, if you've sneezed.'
Oh I'll come back then, I was so relieved.
I left the doctors, feeling crafty
Oh this weather is getting draughty
I'm really shivering, aching too
Oh no! I'm coming down with the flu!

Sue Starling

THE END OF FREEDOM

The last day of the holidays
For child and teacher is so sad.
They've had a taste of freedom's ways,
The road ahead is looking bad.

The child must don a uniform
And be alert in every class.
It's so important to conform
And in exams to earn a pass.

The teacher too, must dress the part
And keep the class under control.
The marking load might break a heart,
But good results are the main goal.

They both must on the treadmill go,
How much they share, they little know.

Ann Nunan

YOU ARE NOT ALONE!

The road you walk on is rocky,
It's hard to grin and bare,
People can't understand how you're feeling,
Life seems so unfair,
You are left feeling empty and confused,
Not knowing what to do,
But just remember friend,
We are all there too,
Each of us are struggling
To find our own way home.
The journey is a long one,
But you are not alone.

H Doidge

DIRE WARNING - NEVER JUMP TO CONCLUSIONS

Once upon a time on a building site,
The labourers laboured by day and by night.
With double time on Sundays and bonuses galore
They very soon reached the 14th floor.

They were indeed a happy bunch
And from 12 to 2 they enjoyed their lunch.
All were carefree, except for Pat -
So now I will tell you the reason for that.

Every day his lunch was the same,
- He said Mrs Murphy was to blame.
Sandwiches of pickles and cheese -
Pickles and cheese every day, if you please.

At last it was more than he could bear.
He said to his friends, 'Begorra, I swear
I'll jump from this floor if it happens once more.'
- And he crossed himself as this oath he swore.

So the following day when the whistle blew,
They waited to see what Pat would do.
They wanted to see the look on his face
When he opened his battered luncheon case.

He opened the lid of his little tin,
And, to his horror on looking therein,
Was a sight that made his very blood freeze,
For lying there was a sandwich - of cheese!

I regret to say, he kept his word,
And, although to you, this may sound absurd,
All pleas for restraint he decided to ignore
And he launched himself from the 14th floor.

Recovering from the after effects,
His friends called round to pay their respects,
As they turned and went away, they heard the widow Murphy say
'That's odd - he made his lunch himself today!'

Reg Windett

THE TRIALS AND TRIBULATIONS OF A DIABETIC CAT

My pussy was quite poorly, so we visited the vet.
An experience that both of us would rather just forget.
She travelled in a cat cage, on the back seat of the car,
Her little heart was racing, though the journey wasn't far.
Arriving at the surgery, I put her on the floor
But a dog came to investigate and frightened her some more.
Upon a hard, cold table, the check-up then took place,
Thermometer inserted, well you should have seen her face
'Cause when she'd cooked it hot enough, it went off with a *ping*.
This modern day technology is such a clever thing.
A torch was shone into her eyes, deficiencies to spot
And then into my clammy hand, was thrust a sample pot.
A specimen of pussy's 'wee', was needed for a test.
I'm sure without much trouble, you can visualise the rest.
So after much hilarity, I clutched my hard earned prize.
When diagnosis was pronounced, imagine my surprise,
A diabetic moggy, most unusual they say
Requiring special diet and injections every day.
Then just to be quite certain, the vampires had to bite
And the blood showed confirmation of the poor old lady's plight.
So a new regime was introduced and insulin begun.
It's got to be the hardest thing that I have ever done.
She didn't take too kindly to the dry high fibre food
And as for those sharp needles, well, I don't think we'll allude.
But we're plodding on regardless, her nine lives to prolong,
For after fifteen cat filled years, together we belong.

Sue MacKenzie

THE MEAL

He looked into his cup
Only to find a hunger
He was determined to try to
Analyse his leanings
And all he got was the other's
Of the crew's way of seeings
For the Frogmats wouldn't wait
For their dinner
Of lettuce and dill sauce.
With beetroot too of course.

Mick Vukasinovic

TWO THOUSAND

This is the year most people have looked forward to
What will be the difference from years before?
Only that we are older, wiser we hope
That's what we are, richer or poor
Health and happiness is what we wish for
Our family and friends near
Understanding, thoughtful and kind
Sympathetic and very dear
Aware of the many changes each year brings
Nothing stays the same, people or things
Dear old England, this is my home.

Vera May Waterworth

My Dog

My dog is called Poppy,
Yes, Poppy is her special name;
She is large and lovely,
So beautiful, always the same.

A beagle, brown, black and white
Is she, and such a faithful pet;
Wonderful colours, such a sight
To see, if ever you have met.

Rescue dog may Poppy be,
Due to a health condition;
But loved is she, dear to me,
As she so fulfils her mission.

She is almost five years old,
Her birthday in November;
Eleventh day, eleventh month,
A special time to remember.

So may God bless her each day,
May she be well, a faithful friend;
As she travels on her way,
So may she always me attend.

Margaret R Bromham

MISTI!

She majestically arranges herself on her pillow of silk:
On her white chin glistens a smidgen of milk -
Her tortoiseshell fur gleams in the sun,
While her green amber eyes sparkle with fun,
Her rasping pink tongue, deftly licks at her fur
Moreover, deep from her throat she emits a loud purr,
Her magnificent tail is her joy and her pride,
While, her thick white ruff is a place where bells can hide,
She closes her eyes, her long lashes rest on her cheeks awhile -
And across her bud like mouth, plays a soft gentle smile,
Her looks are exquisite, and gentle her ways,
I love my pussycat, Misti, knowing with me she always stays!

Linda Gregory

THE MUSICAL BOX

A gift - so many years ago
I felt so proud that I gave to you
It came from Sorrento when I was so small
Where I'd been on holiday having a ball
A musical box that gave so much pleasure
With a beautiful tune to play at your leisure
There it sat for so many years
Next to your bed - but now brings me tears
For now it sits so proudly by
The side of my bed - till the day I die

Janet (Tuthill) Carter

Famous Bits

Dolly Parton has her boobs and Cher has black/blond hair
Elvis Presley had his quiff, Val Doonican his rocking chair
Rod Stewart has his sexy legs, Rolf had a didgeridoo
The Beatles had their screaming fans, the Osmonds had a few

Prince Charlie has his juggie ears, the PM has his grin
Noel Edmonds had his Crinkly Bottom - whatever happened to him?
Sandie Shaw had naked feet
Demis Rousos covered up with a sheet

JY had his radio prog
And Johnnie Noakes had Shep the dog
Charlie Dimmock in her garden bared all
And Beckham was happiest when kicking a ball

Robin Hood stole riches to give to the poor
And dear old Larry Grayson just said, 'Shut that door!'
Dick Emery wore an evening dress
And Postman Pat had a cat named Jess

Robert BP founded scouting for boys
Floella went through the round window to play with the toys
Mike Jackson had skin so white, and a monkey for a pet
Nick Leeson in the banking world got many folk into debt

Sue Ellen Ewing shot JR
And Sinclair invented his C5 car
Ronald Macdonald and his fast food to go
Makes millions of dollars all over the globe

Cinders had a glass slipper and married the charming prince
Alfred Hitchcock of movie fame had several double chins
Richard Branson has scruffy hair
And aeroplanes that fly to who knows where

All of these folks have made their marks on this life
But must go unnoticed as husband or wife
And go along in their own merry way
And don't always get a chance to have their say!

Val Hoare

LOVING KISS

Your kiss is not just an ordinary kiss
It is the kiss of love and life.
When we kiss either here or in the mist
Our love is beyond all life.

That is around us in this mist of confusion and hate,
Sometimes you may think that I don't love you, but I do.
By the way I love you more each day
Oh I hope you know I'll always love you,
And that loving kiss and your tenderness.

Joanne Mills

Follow Your Dream

Follow your dream,
The sky's the limit!
When the road is rough
and the sun's not shining,
only black clouds are ahead
and you just want to curl up in bed . . .
Don't give up, don't look down,
one door may be closing,
but soon you'll find another opening,
a brand new direction for you to take.
The rewards may not be financial
but for job satisfaction and more,
this could be the most exciting thing
that life's treasury box has in store!

Cathy Mearman

FEET

Human feet are in a pair,
At the opposite end to the hair.
Hens feet are a claw,
Cats and dogs four, are a paw.
Horses have hooves,
Pigs trotters, little grooves.
Giraffes seem a mile from the head,
Tin soldiers feet are made of lead.
Cloven are the feet of the sheep,
At a snake, take a peep,
For he has no feet,
He slithers along on his beat.
Keep you feet firmly on the ground,
For life's a merry-go-round.

Janet Degnan

LIFE AS A CARER

Life as a carer can begin when very young
it's not that you have done something wrong.
It can be sister, brother even father or mother
for them you are the one, it can be no other

Life as a carer can begin when you get wed
it's not because of what you may have said.
It can be baby, child or husband and lover
for them you are the one, it can be no other

Life as a carer can begin as you can get old
it's not because you were not advised or told.
Maybe you, could be him, can't cause bother
for them you are the one, it can be no other

B M Attwood

COUNCIL CONUNDRUM

There were once some ladies of Finchley Road,
Who wanted to hang out their washing.
They asked the warden if she could goad,
The council into some action.

The council were helpful and after some time,
They sent two strapping, tall workmen to see
If they could place two poles and a line,
Without too much of a fee.

The workmen came with a joke and a smile,
They drank cups of tea umpteen.
They worked very hard and after a while,
There were the posts with a line in between.

The ladies were pleased and so their resolve
Was to start on their washing next day.
But first they had a problem to solve,
A puzzle to unravel some way.

When you stand five foot nothing in your stocking feet,
And your arms won't reach very high.
To hang up your washing becomes quite a feat,
When the line's way up in the sky.

And so the moral of this tale,
Is to give the council a shout,
To send you down a strapping, tall male
When your washing needs hanging out!

But councils don't do that we know,
So the line was just for watching.
They wouldn't come and put it down low,
It was removed and never used for washing.

P A Greenwood

BRITISH ISLES

Sing a song of sixpence, sing a song of Wales.
Sing a song from morn till night, set music to a traveller's tales.
Sing a song of plenty, sing to feed the poor.
Sing a song of welcome, to the folks next door.
Sing a song of England, Ilkley moor and dales
Visit inns and restaurants, listen to traveller's tales.
Sing a song of Scotland, kilts, bagpipes and drums.
Steeped in ancient history of interest to old and young.
Sing a song of Ireland from across the Irish sea,
With Irish eyes a-smiling for you as well as me.
Sing a song of yesteryear while wandering dale and hill.
Fill one's mind with green fields and moorland heather filled.
Snow on top of mountains with sparkling waterfalls.
Tingling streams through meadowland, set in fine old stone built walls.
A fine old English farm house with honeysuckle round the door,
While set in Scottish Highland a crofter sweeps the floor.
A croft with Scottish magic is like a breath of spring,
Which fills one's heart with gladness and tempts the voice to sing.
Sing a song with Welshman through mountain pass and road,
A gift of love to everyone and a wish to share one's load.
Sing a song of every day with blessings all around.
Sing a song for everyone to share that gladsome sound.

Clarence Gascoigne

THE PAIN GAME

Life is a drain
You are my strain
I feel deep pain

Feelings of misery
Pester me constantly
Feels like thorns
Biting into my skin

We hurt one another
Barking and snarling
Words without meaning,
Sting like a bee.

Why can't we make each other happy?
Is it life's trauma that causes us dismay?
Or is it just a painful game we play?

Lynda Jobling

A Kentish Lad

Across the fields a young boy sprang,
And in and out the hedgerows green,
Quite unaware that all would change,
For him these things had always been.

He watched the river crammed with ships,
Tankers, freighters, tall ships fair,
How could he guess in years to come
That hardly one would e'er pass there?

He strolled along a north Kent way
With English elms high overhead,
But who could tell that four decades
Would see each tree and leaf quite dead?

He wandered down the Mounts Wood Lane,
A lad of 22 or so,
Not dreaming that in future years
Both wood and lane were doomed to go.

The marsh had stood a thousand years,
For birds and fish to thrive upon,
Then someone had a good idea,
And in a year the marsh was gone.

So, by the turning of the Earth,
Or in the blinking of an eye,
Or through a lack of vigilance;
So the thieves go stealing by.

Graham Bloss

FISHING BEACH HYTHE

Close by the Ranges red-flagged guard,
And westward of the promenade,
The fishing boats, proud, crest the beach,
Beyond the wild seas farthest reach.

The boats bedecked with bunting bright,
Secured by hawsers taut and tight.
Backed by black huts that form a screen,
That distant Roughs are seldom seen.

The Lifeboat Station stands forlorn,
Bereft of life, and purpose shorn.
It sent its final boat to work
Upon the beaches of Dunkirk.

The seawards never changing sights
Show distant Folkestone on the heights,
And Dungeness's shingled spit
By intermittent flashing lit.

The daily launchings rough routine
Continues, though the catch is mean;
Decreasing stocks of fish foretell
Their doom, though only time will tell.

Jax Burgess

ALL SUNDAY'S CHILDREN
*(This poem is about the clients with learning disabilities
that I have worked with for over 30 years)*

I live in isolation, craving your warmth and care,
I reach out for your love, I need you always to be there.
A communion of spirit, not a meeting of minds.
Equals in terms of human worth, just be unconditionally kind.
Communicate with me, relate as one to one,
I could so easily have been your daughter or your son.

Glynis Flewin Cooke

INFINITY

I love the sky in all its moods,
How bright it shines, how dark it broods,
Pillows of cloud, in deep blue sky,
Seen from a plane, as above I fly,
So feather soft and white they seem,
I walk upon them, in a dream,
Each step is silent, left then right,
A canopy of blue, a quilt of white,
Then as I walk upon the shore
The skies light up, with sudden roar,
And black clouds scud
As if to run from raging flood
Of pouring rain, and lightnings' flash,
And rush, and bump and tear and crash,
And jagged blinding rips of red,
And orange, yellow, flame-like spread
Across a black and angry sky,
So huge are they, so small am I,
Then in a field of golden corn
I watch a day, so newly born,
A pale sun rises, fresh and damp,
Before the dawn has lit its lamp,
In sky as blue as baby's eyes
All glorious the sun will rise,
The world awakens, birds will sing,
What will this lovely morning bring?

Then, slowly at the close of day,
Before the light has gone away,
Bright bars of gold, and red and blue,
And colours bright of every hue,
Will change, and change before my eyes,

Light up and glorify the skies,
Then as the sun, reluctant, fades,
The night shuts down its velvet shades,
Then lights the stars, like candles bright,
To glint and sparkle through the night.

Margery Crabtree

A Summer Morn

Like an angelic choir singing,
So the birds are bringing
Music to our ears.
The beauty moves us to tears.
Like music from on high,
So the birds cry,
They sing their praises,
Beauty from the dust raises,
As the sun is born,
On this sweet morn.

I T Hoggan

THANK YOU!

We can dance and play and laugh
Eat and drink wonderful things
We can talk and see and think
Listen to music and sing

We can run through grassy fields
And swim through cool brooks
We can see rainbows and stars
And read magnificent books

We can feel the beating of our hearts
And the wind, rain and sun
We can fly above the clouds
And sail many an ocean

Focusing on what is not
Leads to so much pain
Focusing on what we have got
We have so much to gain

Andrea Darling

LIVING WITH ANGELS
For Ian

Oh, my much-loved friend,
Do not leave me for your kindred;
Nor put out the candle before it starts to glow.
Unfurl your angel wings
And teach me how to fly,
Guide me gently, for without you
I will fall.

Place your head,
Here on my breast and listen to
The rhythm of my pounding heart.
One day you will realise that
It beats just for you.
With one cruel word
You could stop it.

Vicky Stevens

THE DANCE OF SPRING

Flaxen hair o'er smooth soft shoulders
Eyes wide open to the summer skies
Slender body of a ballerina
Painted toes in your crimson shoes
Dance the dance of the happy hearted
The world's full of trust and love for you.

The clouds on high they're gently parted
Your arms stretched out like a bird in flight
Valley's below in all their splendour
Awoke to the day when you danced anew.

Ballerina, oh ballerina
Dance the dance of the happy hearted
Throughout the spring until it's parted
Come fill the Heavens with your beauty
Your rays are found in the drops of dew.

You are nature's ballerina
You're new life after winter cruel
You are the petals on a flower
The pirouette of sun and moon.

Come dance the dance of the happy hearted
Throughout the spring until it's parted
Come share yourself with everyone
For lovers love because of you.

Ronald D Lush

TREASURE TROVE

Barley our cat, is the colour of the autumn downs
He is one up on the colours of the other cats in towns
He was born near Brighton's treasure trove
One day a chauffeur driven Rolls Royce arrived from Hove
With a lady and white pussycat inside, going for a ride
Instead they ran over Barley's tail, *not his inside*

Into PDSA Barley was rushed to repair his tail like new
Slowly but surely Barley, poor Barley, began to mew
Did they say there is nothing to pay?
Yes . . . Now Barley sits and purrs all day.

Paff

DUCKLINGS

A little duckling on his own
Looked so appealing - so alone,
My friend and I in generous mood
Searched in our bags to find him food.

We did not know our lonely duck
Was just a scout - he gave a quack
An eager mother-duck soon led
A swarm of ducklings to be fed.

They swam and quacked across the lake -
Our picnic quite inadequate -
We panicked - tried to move away
But, as we moved - well, so did they!

They followed closely at our heels
Quacking their 'hungry duck' appeals.
And we would be there to this day
But passers-by shooed them away

Apparently we had forestalled
Some folks who regularly called
To feed the ducks - so this mayhem
Came, because ducks thought we were them!

The moral here is clear to see
Don't waste on ducks your sympathy
Stem kindly word before it's uttered
Ducks know which side their bread is buttered!

Win Price

MOTHER

Birthday gatherings, Christmas fayre
Lights flicker on bough of tree
Peals of laughter float on air
Enveloped by love bestowed on me.

Gentle kisses heal the hurt
Ceasing instantly the pain
Tender hands brush away the dirt
Revived I join the game again.

Awakened by a haunting dream
Deep into the dark of night
You held me close in candlelight gleam
Until dawn of early morning light.

Life's misfortune came along
You halt my falling tears
Ever stalwart you made me strong
Releasing me from doubt and fears.

If unheeded mine is the blame
Lessons learned in a happy home
Teaching love not wealth or fame
Brings peace of mind where e're you roam.

The warmth of your love surrounds me still
My friend, my rock, my mother
I love you Mam, I always will
Eternally we embrace each other.

Thelma (Slee) Thomas

ADAM AND EVE

Adam and Eve to the garden were sent
Food was cheap and also the rent
But Adam got greedy, wanted to swipe
Eve's green apple before it was ripe.

Daisy Cooper

TEENAGE KICKS

When Jimmy started his first school
The children there were rather cruel.
His clothes were old and far too small,
And just for this the kids would call
Him names and make him play alone,
But you would never hear him moan.
As he grew and years went on,
Jimmy's friends - well he had none.
His clothes were ripped; his shoes were tattered,
Because of this the bullies battered
Jimmy every chance they'd get,
And in fear, his bed he'd wet.
And for the smell, they'd mock him more,
They'd punch and kick him to the floor.
With violent blows, the pain would go,
But the mental scars would grow and grow.
The names they called cut to the core,
His body beat and bruised, was sore.
Unfortunately, things got worse.
'Til from the gates they watched the hearse
Which carried Jimmy's broken shell,
His only freedom from this hell.
His will to live had ebbed away,
Beaten from him day by day.
He took his life. He could not cope.
He had no help. He had no hope.
He left the world a tortured soul.
So did the bullies reach their goal?
Did they think he felt no pain,
As they beat him to his grave?

Joanne Cross

BONNIE, CLYDE AND ACCOMPLICES

The evening started fine,
Carrot soup washed down with wine.
There were four not two!

The next course was served with grace,
Steak, pork, chicken and trout served with mace.
There were four not two!

Desserts came next,
Chocolate mousse, just as you'd expect.
There were four not two!

Coffee liqueurs reasonably priced,
Plus one tea suitably iced.
There were four not two!

Then finally came the bill,
Calculated by a waiter called Phil
It was for *two* not *four!*

The bill was paid in a tick,
And we hurried away right quick.
There were four not two!

As we calculated our saving,
A brave little waitress came raving
"Scuse me' there were *four* not *two!*'

Annette Murphy

Matt Cain

There was a man called Matt Cain
Who left his bike in the rain
He sat in the saddle
And started to paddle
All the way down the lane

Coleen Bradshaw

THE FURRY HAT

While walking in a country lane,
The scent of violets after rain,
Mists clouded the trees around,
The raindrops sparkled on the ground.

A chilly wind rustled the trees,
The man wore his hat against the breeze,
The morn so quiet and supreme,
But quite a shock shattered the dream.

A sudden knock upon his head,
Sent him reeling in a nettle bed,
Gone was his hat, away in the clouds,
A buzzard mistook the furry crown.

Mistaken for a rabbit snack,
The furry hat he wouldn't give back,
Discovering at once his silly mistake,
He dropped it down upon the slate.

The hat was on the roof to stay,
What a beginning to the day!
Only the shriek from the buzzard's call,
Frustrated and hungry that was all.

Eveline Tucker

THE TINY VEGETARIAN

As I pushed my granddaughter on a swing,
She suddenly stopped and ceased to sing.
'Grandma,' she said as she studied her feet,
'How do they make animals into meat?'
Think carefully, Grandma, I said to myself,
How you answer this question is important.
'They are killed first, then cooked,' I replied
As lightly as I could muster.
'But how are they killed while they are alive?
There must be blood,' said my tot under five.
'I don't know, darling,' I said, out of my depth.
'I do,' she said, 'With guns and knives I expect.'
Sadly I wondered what she had watched on TV.
This little girl still only three.
I waited with dread for the next remark,
To come from my granddaughter on a swing in the park.
I must have handled the questions well,
Because she slipped off the swing and broke the spell.
'My mummy and I don't eat animals,' she said.
'We love them too much and eat vegetables instead.'
The truth of this story emerged bye and bye,
'Twas a boy aged ten who had made her cry.
To be a vegetarian was not up his street,
Everyone yes, everyone should eat meat.

Jeanette Middleton

REMEMBER ME

Can you catch my laughter
Floating in the air?
Can you hear me breathing
Sunlight in my hair?
Can you capture love and life
Hold them in your hand?
Can you stop the moments
Which pass like timer sand?

Will you think of me and smile
When I am far away?
Will you love me when I've gone?
If only for a day.
Will you see my face and sigh
'Cos things just aren't the same?
Will you wipe me from your heart
And then forget my name?

Sandi Cooper

THE WINDS OF CHANGE

When you're partially sighted and you can't see much
And you seem to have lost your feminine touch
When you 'mix and match' clothes no longer agree
That shape in the mirror, can that really be me?
Your friends may tell you to wear bright gear
But of being thought gaudy I have a great fear

You put on your vest, but that's front to back
Feels like your wearing a 'high necked' sack
You turn round the vest and put it to rights
Next you struggle and fumble with unending tights
I'd torment the man who invented those
Full marks to designers of easy-wear hose

Step into those knickers with a bow at the front
That hurdle surmounted, give a satisfied grunt
'Flat-chested' I don't have to war with a bra
No one will notice if I'm viewed from afar
Hat and coat donned I complete the test
But where was I going when fully dressed?

It's no fun getting old if you see, or not
What am *I* doing? Well I sleep a lot
Daytime's I'm dozy, whilst at night I'm awake
I wish I'd not tackled that large slice of cake
Still what can you do in your later life
When you've lost all urge for trouble and strife

Yvonne V Smith

SEE THAT GIRL

I see that girl yet just don't see
Why oh why she does not like me
I have given her flowers and lots of sweets
And asked her what is her idea of a treat.

I see that girl yet just don't see
Why she keeps on avoiding me
I see her at work nearly every day
So try and make a joke with everything I say.

I see that girl yet just don't see
Why the police came to see me
I have not hurt her at all
But at work I have not seen her at all.

Keith L Powell

A Schoolboy's Opinion Of Numeracy

Numeracy is boring! Numeracy is fun!
Sometimes I've learnt and sometimes I've not done!
Angles, decimals, bar charts and data!
Once I complained to Miss - and did it later!
Yesterday my head nearly exploded with all these things!
My nostrils were melting, my ears were a-ring!
But when numeracy is over and it's home time from school,
Whatever happens - Numeracy's still cool!

Jeff Goodwin (10)

FEELINGS

You who are in my heart and mind,
Give me reasons to love and be kind,
I would want a friend not foe,
When I open my life's door,
I would want a friend if I had to fight,
Who with wisdom, would do what's right,
If, they expect the same of you and me,
Fight with honour and sincerity.

The spirit of hope and help and love,
The spirit of Heaven up above,
The measure of friendship,
Measured in love,
Depth of meaning,
By the growing of feelings
Faith in the Heavens, up above,
The power of the spirit, you faith and your *love*.

D Davies

The Taxi

The taxi pulls up outside the station
Ready to take people to their destination
The driver sits and waits
Wondering if he has a passenger coming through the gates.

They may be young, they may be old
Perhaps, they're shy or perhaps bold,
Does he worry, does he care?
It matters not as long as they pay the fare.

Suddenly, a figure appears at the door,
'Are you for hire driver?'
'Can you take me where I want to go?'
'Certainly Madam, certainly Sir,
Help with your luggage?'
'No I'll keep them in here.'

The driver he gives the going rate,
'That's fine just get me there mate.'

The taxi moves off down the road,
With paying passenger safely on board.

He looks in the mirror and in anticipation
Slowly engages in small conversation

Finally, the trip is over for both passenger and driver.
'That's three-fifty please.'
'Tell you what, please take a fiver.'

Phillip Walters

IN THE BLINK OF AN EYE

We pass as shadows in the night,
As ships on the high sea.
We touch as waves caress the shore,
As the sun lays upon the sea.
You are a flicker of bright light,
A swirling mist of haze,
Brief as a rainbow in a storm.
We are just merely butterflies,
Flitting on the breeze.
Touching for a moment with our hearts,
And flying on again.
We are but sunrays,
From behind a cloud,
A shadow from a bee.
We are a drop of dew upon the grass,
that soon will fly away.
You are a moonbeam in the darkness,
The slight blink of a small star,
Just a flicker before a cloud does form.
A slight thunderous rumble in the far off distance,
Or the dance of a firefly by night,
Under the stars slight light.

Hannah Inglis

TINY THE TORTOISE

There is a little tortoise who lives beside the sea
He left his home to live alone because he's so tiny
He hides behind the sandcastles to watch the children play
His only friend is a big, blue ball which he plays with every day

When the children have gone he feels all alone
He plays with his blue ball and begins to moan
If only I was bigger, if only, he wished
He thought about it, when he went out and fished

Tiny the tortoise was in the sea when he heard a little cry
A bird flew by, who cried the cry, and Tiny wondered why
Tiny the tortoise got out of the sea and went to see what was wrong
There he became good friends with the bird and they played
                                                              all day long

Like Tiny, the bird had also left home
'I'm just far too loud!' he said with a groan.
But that didn't matter to Tiny, Bird was his only friend
He doesn't need his blue ball anymore because their friendship
                                                              will never end.

Sadie-Louise Berry

Goodnight Sweetheart

We had to buy another bed
So I could rest my weary head
Into the next room, close the doors
To get away from the awful snores

Will someone please - doctor or nurse
Find a cure for this terrible curse
It's much worse now that he's getting older
The snores have become so much bolder!

It starts at one on the Richter Scale
I kick him, I punch him to no avail
When it builds up to three I get up and make tea.
By number eight I am usually wide-awake
Listening to sounds like a small earthquake!

They put men on the moon, educate a baboon
And fly around the world in an air balloon
So why can't a scientist invent a device
To save the sanity of this poor wife!

Pamela Porter

MISERY

Where do I go with this powerful blight
the one that torments me from morning to night,
starving myself to retain all the power,
leaving me looking like a wilted, dead flower?

There are two sides to my secret life:-
To let a morsel pass my lips, swallow all the strife,
facing the public scorn, along with all the stigma,
why can't she just eat? A powerful enigma!

I'd like to be normal, as free as a bird,
to shine like a superstar, instead of coming third,
I try with all my might, to release myself from this,
I've known it all my life, what you've never had, you don't miss.

Perhaps I'm trying to kill myself, in my deep private hell,
to gain the ultimate in control, only time will tell.
To forget the past, break through, be free,
just begs one question, does anyone understand me?

H E Hanson

MISSING YOU

I called out for you last night
But you were not there
I'll call out again tonight
For you, if I dare.

Please be there for me tonight
You know I'm missing you
I know you always cheer me up
When I'm feeling blue.

When you come I'll be ready
Laying in my bed
Sleeping so sound and steady
With you running through my head.

If you visit me each night
Time will fly I'm sure
And before we both know it
You'll be knocking at the door!

Roger Stevens

THE STILLNESS OF GRACE

The deep calm that is beauty's face,
Is the stillness of grace.
As the night descends
From evening that lends
Its wings to fly,
Into the twilight sky.
Silence from the dying sun
As the moon comes.
The deep calm that is beauty's face
Is the stillness of grace.

I T Hoggan

BIG KIDS ON KIDS

Big kids today,
They don't know what to do,
That's complete with computer,
And a PlayStation two.

They moan that they are bored,
While hanging around the park.
But try and get them in,
Before that it gets dark.

When I was a child,
I made do with my bike,
And if things got really bad,
We made a den in the back dyke.

When they hang around in groups,
People think that they are thugs,
And then they get a bad name,
As people think they're on drugs.

Most of them are sensible,
And go to Youth Club,
But you always get the odd few,
That would rather go to the pub.

But then that's big kids today,
They think they know what's best,
But really they've a lot to learn,
So give us parents a rest!

Linda Berry

The High Chair

Covered in dust in the attic it stood,
The old high chair, made with love and wood.
Not alone - far from that it's true
There were suitcases - matching - in blue,
An umbrella stand and boxes galore,
Even a sideboard - with a missing door
A pair of wellies and a summer hat,
A basket with a blanket -
A bed for a cat.
The high chair was the saddest of that clan
The boy had grown up and was now a man.
The old folk had moved - the house was too big
With a great big garden for two to dig.
It missed a chubby tot on it's seat
It's legs being kicked by tiny feet.
In another time, on another day
A mushy dinner stood on its tray
Then - one day in spring a couple came
The chair wasn't interested in their name
The lady couldn't get in the attic at all
She was heavy expecting and not very tall.
Then early in summer the day came round
When the high chair heard a joyful sound.
He knew it well, he'd heard it before
The baby's cry, through the attic door.
Then on a day when it was pouring with rain
Back to the attic the young man came
When he first looked in he'd noticed it there
They need it now, this nice old chair.
After the baby was tucked in bed
He took the chair to the garden shed.
He scrubbed it well, and thought it quaint
And decided to give it a coat of paint.
Lemon or blue? What colour? What kind?
Then after a while he changed his mind.

That lovely wood - so old and mellow
Underneath a coat of yellow?
Then another idea came in his head
And he gave it a coat of varnish instead.
Now he was pleased with the job he'd done,
The chair was ready for his baby son.
The dad said, 'Well son, what do you think?'
Could the chair be mistaken - did he see the boy wink?

Dottie Bond

THE 'GIFT' TO THE WORLD

They come into this life
as perfect little beings
pure in thought and character
untouched, unspoiled, a gift.

Some are raised in strife
others deprived of basic things
lucky ones are given better
loved, nurtured, a life.

Which ones will take up the knife?
Who has the chance to spread their wings?
Which ones will really matter?
Yours, mine, theirs?

Children belong to us all!

Christine Anne Davies

House Buyer's Lament

I'd like to buy a house,
But property prices are to high.
But I can't raise enough money to do it,
However hard I try.
I've reduced my expenditure to the bone,
I've got no electricity or gas,
I've had them disconnect the phone.
What makes me very angry,
And makes me really see red.
I can't even raise a deposit,
To put down on an ordinary garden shed.
I've come to the conclusion,
That I shall always have to rent.
The only thing that I could afford,
Would be a very cheap one man tent.

F Pelton

ANCHOR BOOKS
SUBMISSIONS INVITED
SOMETHING FOR EVERYONE

ANCHOR BOOKS GEN - Any subject, light-hearted clean fun, nothing unprintable please.

THE OPPOSITE SEX - Have your say on the opposite gender. Do they drive you mad or can we co-exist in harmony?

THE NATURAL WORLD - Are we destroying the world around us? What should we do to preserve the beauty and the future of our planet - you decide!

All poems no longer than 30 lines.
Always welcome! No fee!
Plus cash prizes to be won!

Mark your envelope (eg *The Natural World*)
And send to:
Anchor Books
Remus House, Coltsfoot Drive
Peterborough, PE2 9JX

**OVER £10,000 IN POETRY PRIZES
TO BE WON!**

Send an SAE for details on our New Year 2003 competition!